WITHDRAWN
UST
Libraries

The Making of a Newspaper Man

By

SAMUEL G. BLYTHE

GREENWOOD PRESS, PUBLISHERS
WESTPORT, CONNECTICUT

Reprinted from an original copy in the collections
of the Yale University Library

Originally published in 1912
by Henry Altemus Company, Philadelphia

First Greenwood Reprinting 1970

Library of Congress Catalogue Card Number 76-95085

SBN 8371-3075-1

Printed in the United States of America

The Making of a Newspaper Man

CHAPTER I

THERE was to be a murder trial at the little county-seat where I was born and where I lived as a boy. I was just eighteen at the time. Murder trials were infrequent in that county and this one attracted wide local attention. The city papers were preparing to give some space to it and the county papers had printed columns about it.

It was the first murder trial I remember much about, though when I was a small boy they hanged a man in the jailyard, which enlivening and novel occurrence had set all the small boys in the village to making gallows and hanging cats and dogs, and even fieldmice and rabbits.

Once we built a big gallows and tried to hang a calf, but that didn't work very well—and the man who owned the calf caused some acute discomfort to the amateur executioners. Until he caught me, I never realized how much power there is concealed in the human leg and foot when the foot is shod with a cowhide boot. Still, murder trials and murders were always a fruitful topic of boyish conversation. Instead of using a trap for the condemned man to fall through to eternity, the local plan was to jerk him into the hereafter by means of a big weight fastened to a rope running over the top of the gallows and released by a spring. The weight was an iron affair and the tradition was that it weighed three hundred and sixty-five pounds. At any rate, it was kept in the cellar of the courthouse; and as the frequent sheriffs always had boys in their families the cellar of the courthouse was a favorite place of resort. Consequently, when conversation languished, the weight was always there to furnish inspiration for speculation as to whom it would be used on next and the coördinated and congenial theme of murders and murderers.

Of course, having arrived at the mature age of eighteen, I had long since ceased foregathering in the court-house cellar and trying to lift the weight and discussing murders and the last hanging; but when this case was moved for trial, and the farmers began to come in, I was as much interested as I had been in the hanging of the unfortunate years before, and so were all my companions and friends. Our nearest city was thirty miles away and the daily papers came in on the morning and evening trains. They devoted one page to the news of the country through which they circulated and had correspondents in each village of importance. The correspondent for the biggest of the morning papers from our town was a young lawyer, a warm friend of mine. It so happened he had other business to attend to at the time of the trial and he asked me to report it for the city paper.

My father was editor of one of the two weekly

papers in our town, and naturally I had fussed about the printing office a good bit. Moreover, I always received better marks for compositions than the other boys, and my rhetoric teacher had prophesied a great future for me. Also, I had secretly determined to be a newspaper man, although my father objected strenuously, saying the business was no good. So, when the regular correspondent asked me to do his work, I jumped eagerly at the chance. The arrangement was that I was to have the pay for the work that he would have received had he done it. The emolument for the literature of country correspondence in that particular city newspaper office was four dollars a column, which seemed a princely compensation, for I was to have a front seat at the reporters' table, was to hear the whole trial; and likely as not there would be some city reporters there with whom I might get acquainted and thus find an opportunity to discuss my ambition to be a regular reporter myself. I would have worked for nothing.

The trial began on Monday, and I made a longhand running report of the proceedings, got it in the afternoon mail and telegraphed a short, skeletonized summary of what happened after the mail closed. I have filed several million words of telegraphic dispatches to newspapers since that day, twenty-five years ago, from all parts of the world and on all sorts of big stories; but I have never filed a dispatch that seemed quite as important and sensational as that. I was all puffed up when I handed it to the telegraph operator, who had known me since I was a baby, and she was greatly interested and promised to send it right away. Likewise, I have dealt with and known hundreds of telegraph and cable operators in my time, have fought with them, coaxed them, cursed them, bought them, cultivated them, loafed with them; but that dear lady who sent my first newspaper dispatch, while I hung around nervously waiting to see her finish it, remains in my mind as the highest type of the exponents of the business which I was to be so interested in in later life.

Telegraph operators have befriended me, have balked me, have put my stuff ahead and given me highly useful information to my great credit in the home office, and have held back my dispatches to my great discredit in the same important place; they have endangered their jobs to pull me through and have cost me a job or two by utter cussedness. Some of the best fellows I ever knew were in the telegraph business, and are yet; but never a one of them did so much for me, I still think, as the lady who sent my first two hundred words and told me it was quite intelligent.

I was at the post-office next morning an hour before the papers came, and when they finally did arrive I grabbed the first one I could get. I was much chagrined to find that news of Congress and the Legislature and a prize fight were prominently displayed on that first page. There wasn't a line about the murder trial. I hurried in to consult the postmaster and asked him if he was sure my letter got away. He was sure and suggested it was possible the murder-trial story might be on some other page of the paper than the first. I hadn't thought of that. It had never occurred to me that my dispatch could possibly be any other place than on the first column of the first page. I have had that feeling a good many times since, too.

I found the dispatch on page three, two columns, with a four-line head. I read it eagerly, lamenting a few typographical errors, and feeling much discouraged because the editors had cut out half a column or so of the very best part—as I thought. The papers came in at nine o'clock in the morning and court began at ten. I spent that hour swelling around on Main Street, feeling quite sure everybody had read my story, and thinking perhaps the judge and the lawyers would say something about it. Besides, it meant almost eight dollars in money for me—a sum I had never thought any person could make for a day's work. Also, it clinched me for the newspaper business. I was a born journalist. There was no doubt of that. And it was a cinch. Eight dollars for a few hours' work that was really play! Nobody in the village made so much working for wages.

I worked my head off that week and sent in columns that were printed and columns that were not. In the evenings I went to the hotel and talked to the city reporters who were on the story. Much to my surprise, they didn't think newspaper work was a noble profession, highly paid, dignified and supremely important. They said reporting was "darned hard work," that the pay was small and the hours long. Also, they said—all of them—their city editors were individually and collectively the meanest men on earth, and it was a poor game all round. Later, I entertained the same ideas, especially about the city editors, and had the same ideas entertained, quite extensively, about me when I became a city editor myself. I made almost sixty dollars that week—more than I was to make in many a weary week afterward—and had my story on the first page the day the man on trial went on the stand.

CHAPTER II

On Saturday a man who was employed on a Sunday paper in the city where my paper was published—I had begun to talk of it as "my" paper—came to get a story for Sunday morning. I didn't know it then, but that man was to cross and crisscross my life for several years —principally cross. He sat next to me at the table, and asked me if I was the "yap" who had been doing the trial for the "Gazette." I said I was. "Pretty good for a rube!" he commented. I had asked the other city reporters about the chance for getting a job as a regular on the staff of some paper in the city. They told me jobs were scarce, that the penurious proprietors always filled up with a cheap jay from some college when a high-priced man was fired, and advised me, unanimously and profanely, to stick to the village or go on a farm.

It was a rotten business, anyhow, they said—and nothing, positively nothing, in it.

Still, the man from the Sunday paper seemed to have different ideas. He was older. He told me he had been in the business for fifteen years and was writing a book about it—a guide for aspirants. Of the book, more later; but I asked him if there was any chance to get a job. He told me confidentially there was going to be a shakeup on the paper I was reporting the trial for; that he was going back over there as city editor, and that it wouldn't hurt any to go down and apply. He said he would put in a good word for me.

I could hardly wait for that trial to finish, although I was making six and eight dollars a day out of it. On the day after I sent in my last batch of copy I took the morning train to the city and hurried up to the newspaper office. I had often stood outside that office, which sheltered the biggest paper in the city and one of the biggest in the state, and wondered if ever I should get a chance to work on it and learn the business there. I asked a man in the counting room where the editor's office was. He looked at me curiously and told me it was up another flight. I climbed up, with my heart beating like a pneumatic riveter.

There was a door with frosted glass in it at the top of the dark stairs, and on the door the magic words "Editorial Rooms" were painted. This was about half past eight in the morning. I knocked on the door. Nobody came. Then I pushed it open and found myself in a long room with the floor littered with torn newspapers, proofsheets, copy paper and all the numerous evidences of work the night before. Nobody was there.

I noticed a little coop in one corner of the room that held a desk and chair, and at the far end three other rooms. The doors to these rooms were labeled: "Managing Editor," "Editor" and "Editorial Writers." The long room was crowded with old desks, and along one side there was a table built against the wall, on which there were heaps of the local papers.

That table was where we used to sleep when we were stuck for the long watch. I thought it a particularly untidy and uninviting place then. Six months later it often seemed to me the softest bed in the city. The door of the little coop in the corner of the big room was labeled "City Editor." I knew dimly he was the man I wanted to see.

I sat down and waited. Presently a boy came in and made a pretense of sweeping up the floor. He was not an attractive boy and not much younger than myself. He looked at the littered room with supreme disgust.

"These dubs must 'a' bin brought up in a barn," he said, "the way they throw stuff around."

"What dubs?" I ventured.

"These reporters," he answered. "They gimme a pain! Whatchu want?"

"I want to see the editor," I answered with such dignity as I could command.

He stopped sweeping. "Somethin' wrong in d' pape?" he asked in a more respectful tone.

"I suppose some of them dubs has bin gittin' the wrong dope."

"No," I replied. "I want to get a position on the staff."

"Nothin' doin'," he asserted. "They's firin' instid of hirin'."

Then he went on sweeping and paid no further attention to me. I sat there for nearly three hours and not a person came into that room except another boy with a big bunch of newspapers. He threw them on a desk and walked out. It hadn't occurred to me that the paper I wanted to work for was a morning paper and that the men worked at night and slept in the daytime. That occurred to me a good many times later, but it didn't dawn on me then. I fancied it must be a snap to work there. They didn't go on until afternoon apparently; and, as everybody quit at six o'clock where I came from, that would mean only a short day. If I could only get a job I knew I should have an easy time.

About noon the door was pushed violently

open and a short man with a gray mustache came in. He was not much more than five feet tall, but he had a massive head and one of the most intelligent faces I have ever seen. He glanced at me and went into the room marked "Editor." I heard him moving about the room, and heard him also shout: "Oh, boy!" No boy came. He shouted again. Then he said, "Damn those boys! They are getting worse all the time!" and came out into the room where I was sitting. He looked round, took a copy of the morning paper from a desk and went back. If he noticed me at all I wasn't aware of it.

Nobody came in for another half hour. I could hear the man in the other room swinging back and forth in his chair, could hear newspapers rustling, hear him thump the desk a couple of times and knew from other sounds he was clipping things out of papers. Then I decided I might just as well talk to him as the city editor, who probably didn't get down for an hour or two; and I went timidly into his office. He was tilted away back in his chair, reading a paper and chewing vigorously on something I learned afterward was paper, for I saw him tear strips of it and put them into his mouth.

"Are you the editor?" I asked.

"Yes," he said, peering at me over the top of the paper. "What do you want?"

"I want a job," I blurted.

"What kind of a job?"

"I want to be a reporter."

He had dropped the paper and was looking at me not unkindly.

"Have you ever had any experience?"

"No, sir—that is, not much. I have written some for my father's paper and I reported that murder trial for you."

He was interested.

"Are you the man who reported that murder trial?"

"Yes, sir."

"Well," half to himself, "that wasn't so bad —not so bad. What's your name?"

I told him and he scribbled it down. "All

right," he said, picking up his paper and smiling at me pleasantly, "I'll speak to the city editor about it. You will hear from him. Good morning."

I suppose I walked out of that room, but I don't know. It seemed to me I floated out and down those dingy stairs. I was certain I should get a place—and I caromed round the city in a dream until it came traintime.

When I got home I told my father I thought I could get a place on the local staff of the "Gazette." He shrugged his shoulders. "All right," he said; "but it's a poor business." For the next two days I was the first person at the post-office at mailtime and the last to leave. Then came a letter in the morning mail on the third day. It was from the city editor and said the editor had spoken to him of me; that there was a vacancy on the local staff I could have; that if I wanted it I was to report to him a week from the following Sunday morning. The salary, he added, would be ten dollars a week.

I dashed down the street to my father's office. "I've got it," I shouted to him as I burst into his office.

"Got what?" he asked.

"Got a job on the 'Gazette.'"

"God help you!" he said, and turned to his writing.

CHAPTER III

Money is never particularly plentiful in the family of a country editor and our family was no exception. However, my friend, the young lawyer who had let me sub for him on the murder trial and who thus had really secured my job for me, advanced me some out of his scanty store on the check he would get for me at the end of the month; and at two o'clock on Sunday week—exactly on the minute—I walked again into that big room. I had been hanging round the foot of the stairs for an hour for fear I might be late.

There was a man in the little coop in the corner, writing in a black-covered book. Six or seven young men were sitting in the long room, smoking and talking about a scoop the opposition paper had that morning. They paid no attention to me. I stood for a minute and listened to them. From what I could gather it seemed certain there would be a hot time when the managing editor came in. Presently the man in the coop looked up and saw me.

"Do you want to see me?" he asked.

"I want to see the city editor."

"Go ahead," he said. "I am that unfortunate person." I guessed he was thinking about the scoop, too.

I told him my name and showed him his letter to me.

"How do?" he said, sticking out his hand. "I'll have an assignment for you presently."

Then he took me out into the big room and introduced me to the men there. They all greeted me pleasantly—and one man, older than the rest, with much cordiality. I didn't know why then, but I soon learned. My advent relieved him of the necessity of writing the local notices—the most despised job on the paper.

"Here's the trouble!" sang out the city editor, and the men all flocked round and looked at the black-covered book in which he was writing when I first came in. That black-covered book was the assignment book, and opposite each man's name were his assignments for the day. I waited until the men had copied off their tasks and then looked for mine. I was to see the colonel of a local regiment that had returned from camp that morning and get a story, and I was to report a sermon at night. Also, opposite my name was "local notices."

I noticed that one man was assigned to do "police," another "railroads," another "hotels," and so on. I soon learned there were regular men on these assignments, as on "courts and city hall" on weekdays, and "politicians" and "theatres," and so on; and I wondered when I should get a chance at "theatres" or "police," feeling myself well qualified to cope with either or both right off the bat. However, it wasn't long until I found out it would be some time before I got theatres or police, or anything but the dub assignments. No matter what I thought of my own abilities, the city editor positively refused to consider me except as a dub, who must be taught—and I am quite sure he was right, looking back at it now.

The reporters interested me. Aside from the city reporters who were up in my village on the murder trial, they were the first real reporters I had ever seen. They were young, energetic, free-and-easy chaps, with a most amazing—to me—knowledge of all that was going on in the city, with the most contemptuous opinion of the big-wigs of the place of whom I had read for years and whom I imagined to be most remarkable citizens, free of opinion, full of youth and youthful cynicism, calling big politicians and city officials and merchants and others of the prominent by their first names, cocksure of every statement and bored by things that were new and marvelous to me. They all smoked and most of them drank a little. They knew the night life as well as the day life. They spoke familiarly with policemen and firemen. They knew the café-keepers and all the local characters of whom I had been reading—knew them intimately, it seemed—and disapproved of most of them. I wondered if I should ever get to the dizzy height of calling the chief of police "Jim" and referring to the mayor as "Cornie."

What an underpaid, happy-go-lucky, careless and, in the case of several, brilliant crowd it was! Not one of them had a cent, or expected to have one, except on payday. All lived from hand to mouth. All worked fourteen, sixteen, seventeen hours a day at the most grueling work, reporting on a paper in a small city where many yawning columns must be filled each day whether there is anything going on or not, and all loyal to the core to that paper, fighting its battles, working endlessly to put a scoop over on the opposition morning paper, laboring until four o'clock in the morning for from ten to fifteen dollars a week, doing anything that came along from a state convention to a church wedding.

Everything was grist that came to that mill and those boys were the millers. They are scattered now to all parts of the earth. Some have stuck to the newspaper business and some have left it; but they were a brave crowd of youngsters then and they took me up and made me one of them, and taught me the rudiments of my business. I worked with and against the best reporters in this country and abroad for many years, but I never found a crowd like that—my first colleagues, with whom I lived and borrowed and played and worked when I was both a cub and a dub—good friends, good reporters, good fellows!

I went up to see the colonel of the returned regiment. Much to my surprise, he did not seem awed when I told him so distinguished a journalist as a reporter for the "Gazette" had vouchsafed to call on him, but asked rather shortly, "Well, what do you want?" I told him and he gave me a long story, detailing the splendid achievements of his command and not omitting his own great part in the success of the affair. I hurried back to the office and wrote until my arm ached. When I turned in my copy the city editor looked at the bale of it and said: "Gosh! What did he do? Kill somebody? I only wanted a couple of sticks."

"You wait," I thought, "until you see how important that article is and then you'll change your opinion." However, he didn't wait. With a sick heart, I saw him throw page after page of it on the floor. Next morning they printed about three inches of my article and not much of it resembled what I had written. That was a jolt, but I had a harder one. The sermon I was to report was by a returned missionary bishop. I argued that, inasmuch as they wanted a report at all, they must want a good one, and I labored hard making notes of the sermon and in transcribing them at the office. Then I got my second lesson. Sermons are covered only because nothing else much goes on in a small city on Sunday—or were in my cub days; and if any live news comes in the sermons are cut down. Some live news came in that night—a police case that involved somebody well known; and next morning my report of the sermon was reduced about ninety per cent. when it appeared in type.

I didn't get to my room until four o'clock that

morning, but I got up at seven and went out and bought a copy of the paper. I turned eagerly to the local pages and found my two little items. I was the proudest boy in the United States. To be sure they had not appreciated my articles at their full worth; but they printed some of them right in the paper, in the local sections, and I was a regular reporter on a regular paper! I wouldn't have traded jobs with Charles A. Dana! I thought everybody was pointing me out as the brilliant young journalist of the "Gazette" as I walked down to the office, where, by the way, I arrived three hours ahead of time and occupied my leisure in reading and rereading my contributions to the sum of the world's wisdom that morning. I have them yet, pasted in a scrapbook—two gems of English literature! Nothing I have ever read or written compares with those two items—the one about the regiment and the other about the missionary bishop.

CHAPTER IV

I soon discovered that all the ideas I had about the ease and dignity of the work of a reporter on a daily paper in a small city were entirely erroneous. We reported at the office at one o'clock and took our afternoon assignments. These we were expected to have covered and the copy in before six. We reported again at seven-thirty and got our night assignments, and the copy for those was to be in by eleven or twelve. Then the proofs began coming and nobody could go until the last local proof was read and revised. This was generally about one or half past. Then the long-watch man stayed until four, catching that assignment two or three times a week and watching the police station and the fire alarm for any late crime or fire that might occur.

Expense bills were carefully scrutinized. No

NEWSPAPER MAN 29

reporter was supposed to take a street car if his assignment was within a mile of the office unless there was a great rush, and all street cars stopped at midnight. Thus, if there was a late fire the reporter who had it was expected to run his mile and run back in time to catch the last form. If the fire was over a mile away, in a dangerous district, the city editor would allow a cab, but not too often, for the old man downstairs thought cabs and reporters not compatible with the economical conduct of his great organ of public opinion and instruction.

Naturally the new man on the staff was given the drudgery. He had to hold copy on proof and read the revises. He was stuck with the long watch oftener than anybody else. There were seven reporters and each man had a day off, thus leaving six to get all the news in a city of almost a hundred thousand people, and, as the paper was a big one, to write enough stuff to fill twenty-five or thirty columns—and sometimes more. I frequently had fourteen or fifteen assignments in a day—not big ones, but fourteen or fifteen places that had to be visited, whether they produced copy or not.

Then there were the "local notices." How we hated those! They were advertisements, in news-paragraph style, that ran from five to fifteen lines each and were inserted on the local pages. Each day had its quota and tabs telling what was to be written each day hung on hooks in the city editor's room. They were for shoe stores, drug stores, all kinds of stores; and the advertising man guaranteed they would be "bright and snappy." Think of working all the afternoon and writing two columns of stuff, and then being obliged to go to the hook, get the tabs and write "bright and snappy" items about Beegin's shoes and Boogin's bread, running from five to fifteen lines! Those "local notices" gave me my first pause about the desirability of the newspaper business as a career.

Ten dollars a week, with no other revenue, is not a princely income. Still, under the coaching of my brethren, who were living on it, I soon learned how to stretch that ten dollars to cover seven days. There was a good place where they sold you for three dollars a ticket which entitled you to twenty-one meals. Inasmuch as we all slept late, we had an arrangement whereby the landlady left a luncheon on the table at midnight in lieu of breakfast. That settled the eating problem. By bunking together, two men could get a pretty fair room in those days for four dollars, or two dollars each. That used up half of the ten, but it provided the sterner necessaries. There was a friendly tailor who would make you a suit of clothes for twenty-six dollars —a dollar down and a dollar a week. I never knew how he did it; but that tailor had things calculated to such a nicety that at the end of the twenty-six weeks it was absolutely necessary to buy a new suit or have the old one drop off you in tatters—and we were always in debt to him. Taking out the tailor's dollar—which we did not always do, by the way—we had four dollars left for riotous living, shoes, laundry, tobacco and everything else. Of course some of the boys got twelve dollars and one or two fifteen. The city editor was a plutocrat—he got twenty-five; and the assistant city editor, who was a reporter every day except the city editor's day off, got seventeen.

I remember the day I drew my first week's salary. The assistant city editor was at the cashier's window with me. The cashier, who was a good fellow and would advance a dollar or two in case of dire necessity, shoved our envelopes out face down. They were small manila envelopes, with the name of the recipient written across the middle and the sum within in figures on the upper left-hand corner. I took my ten with a fluttering heart. It was my first salary as a regular reporter. It meant, too, that I had made good enough to last a week, at any rate, and probably could worry through another week. The assistant city editor ostentatiously turned his envelope over and showed me that magnificent "$17.00" on the corner. It was wealth beyond compare. "My boy," he said in a very patronizing manner, "if you ever get so you can pull down that much you will be a real newspaper man." I thought so too.

The city editor earned his twenty-five dollars. In addition to giving out the assignments and being responsible for the local, he was supervisor of the sporting pages and the theatrical news, read all the copy—there were no such persons as copy-readers then in the small cities—wrote the headlines, made up his pages and took the kicks from the managing editor when the opposition scooped us. He was a busy young person, with a sour view of life and an inordinate desire for something that was exclusive, by which he meant something the other morning paper did not have. Likewise, he was always embroiled in bitter warfare with the foreman of the composing room, who was constantly trying to leave out some of his local, and as constantly at odds with the reporters, each of whom fought always to get space for his particular story or stories and gloomed darkly and talked of the decadence of the game when the city editor told him to make a quarter of a column of the yarn he hoped to write a column about.

Everybody was eager and enthusiastic. All were bound up in their paper. They growled and talked privately of the penuriousness of the proprietor, and the cussedness of the city editor, and the malignant managing editor, and the feeble-mindedness of the editor; but they were ready and willing to fight when anybody else intimated their paper was not the greatest in the state. They worked incredibly hard for pittances, walking miles and miles in snow and rain and heat, and toiling long hours through the night; but their complaints were all among themselves. To outsiders they were a gay and debonair bunch of young chaps, engaged in getting out the best paper of them all; and they took as much joy in "putting one over" on the opposition paper as they would in getting a thousand-dollar legacy. It was a good atmosphere to begin in. Likewise, it gave an experience of all sides of the business; for there wasn't a man in the lot who couldn't write heads, read proof, read and edit telegraph, make up, write advertising, write special articles and do any story passably well, no matter whether it was about a prize fight or a church convention.

The routine assignments were divided under broad general heads. There was a police man, a court man, a railroad man—and so on. My first regular assignment was "railroads, undertakers and morgue." That meant that I was expected, in addition to any other assignments the city editor might wish me to cover, to visit all the railroad offices; go to the station when the big trains were due; go to the big undertakers and copy the death certificates; visit the morgue twice a day to see if any bodies were there and where they came from. It meant, also, a walk of six or seven miles each afternoon, for no reporter could use a street car, except at his own expense, on a routine assignment.

The city wasn't much of a railroad centre; so my duties consisted in visiting the railroad offices, where the agents invariably tried to hand out advertisements about excursions and such in the guise of news—and rarely had any real news—and visiting the stations and talking to the station master and dispatchers and other officials. These visits usually resulted in the exciting information that "Mr. McGuffin's special car, Lotus, went east on Number Seventeen last night," though every time the brakeman or engineers or anybody else gave an excursion or a picnic I was expected to boom it for days. Then, after the little grist of local railroad items—occasionally there was a good story—I read the exchanges and clipped a dozen or so railroad items of general interest, which were pasted up and followed the local news under a headline like "Clicks from the Rails," or some other nifty caption.

Unless the death certificate was of some important person, when it was necessary to hunt up facts for an obituary, the news secured at the undertaker's shop was written in stereotyped form, giving the name, age, time of death and place of funeral of the deceased. These were run under a standing headline, "The Dead."

There were about twenty undertakers who must be visited each day, in widely separated sections of the city. If you took a chance and skipped one it was always certain the opposition railroad, undertakers-and-morgue man would visit that identical place that day and get a prominent death good for a spread obituary. After I had been on this run for a week I nearly lost my job by writing an obituary of some esteemed person and leaving out his name. It got into the paper that way and the scholarly managing editor threw fits and profanity all over the office.

CHAPTER V

It was before the days of typewriters or linotype machines and my writing was bad. How I envied one of our reporters who wrote a perfect hand and turned in copper-plate copy! He was a great favorite with the printers and used to go up to the composing room and swap stories with them; while, whenever I went through those sacred precincts, the printers used to rap with their composing sticks on their cases, an emphatic and disconcerting sign of typographical disapproval. One day the foreman reported in the local room that Shorty Anderson, a printer, had thrown a "take" of my copy back on his desk, contemptuously saying: "I can't set that junk! It ain't copy. It's music—and I ain't got no music characters in my case." And another time the chapel held a meeting to protest against my copy; but here Shorty

Anderson was my friend. I had supplied him with a convivial Latin motto for the saloon of a friend of his, and he came to the rescue, urging that the young fellow be given a chance. So I wasn't discharged.

Presently a new man came on and the city editor passed the railroads, undertakers and morgue and the local notices to him. I was given police and soon was on terms of easy familiarity with the chief—whom I called "Jim"—the captains, the lieutenants and the detectives. We discussed crime learnedly—but I soon learned that the idea of the police was to print nothing about what happened in a criminal way until they had "investigated"; and as I broke this rule several times they came to look on me with suspicion, and it was necessary to get another reporter to do "police." I had become reasonably expert at proofreading and could write my own headlines. Our biggest head, except on a most sensational story, was what we called a four-head—a line, a pyramid, another line and a twenty-word pyramid to close it up. The first four-head of which I was really proud was over the story of the death of a telegraph lineman. His name was Finnegan and he fell off a pole. I remember the first two parts of the head and I thought it looked fine in print:

FATAL FOR FINNEGAN

Fearful Fall of Fully Fifty-Five Feet!

The long watch lasted until four o'clock in the morning, which was the time the presses started. All the rest left about two o'clock, unless there was a penny-ante game going, which there usually was after the proofs were all done. The long-watch man was expected to go over to the central police station twice and see if anything had happened. There was a fire-alarm gong in the office. On snowy or rainy nights we usually took a chance and called up the police station by telephone. On nights when we were very tired, as we usually were, the long-watch man stretched out on the file table along the side of the room and went to sleep, relying on the friendly night man at the station to call up if anything happened. One night when I had the long watch I went to sleep on the files and went home at half-past four thinking all was well. It so happened that shortly after our own presses started that morning one of our pressmen fell off the press and broke his neck. The full story appeared in the opposition paper, but our paper had never a word—and the accident happened in our own building! I never quite understood how I held on to my job after that— but I did. However, I heard a few things about myself from the managing editor.

Naturally, in so small a city, there was not enough purely local news to fill the many columns set aside for local in our paper, and each week each reporter was ordered to write two or three "specials," which were stories of a semi-news nature or on any interesting topic or thing that had come under his attention. If they could be made humorous so much the better. This was great training for young writers. We produced all sorts of yarns and I got to be pretty good at it, having a fertile imagination and being new to the city, where odd things the others passed by attracted me.

Also, I worked off some of the compositions the rhetoric teacher had commended. We had one star man at this sort of thing, although most of the specials turned in and printed were very fair as newspaper copy, and some were brilliant. I remember my pride in this star man, as the youngest member of the staff, when he put over his famous "Mystery of Lock Sixty-Six" series. He got a hand and arm of a dead man from a medical student he knew and chopped off several fingers and cut the arm in two or three pieces. Then he went out to Lock Sixty-Six on the canal and dropped in a finger, shortly afterward discovering said finger floating in the water. He came back and wrote a masterly story about his discovery. He speculated graphically on the problems of where the finger came from, whose finger it was and why the police had not reported a missing man. The police, by the way, pooh-poohed the whole story.

Next day he found two more fingers and whooped it up again. The police were stirred. The other papers took it up. Next day he dropped in and took out a section of an arm; and when his third story appeared the entire police department was running round in circles and the people were excited. I can see him now, writing his story, smoking an old cob pipe, with a section of that dead arm propped up on his desk before him. Then, at the end, he explained it all and made the police ridiculous.

Once a circus came to town on Sunday to show on Monday. On Monday morning we had a sensational story about the escape of a blood-sweating behemoth of Holy Writ, telling how this ferocious animal had broken out of his cage and ravaged the countryside. Most of the town went down to see and hunt the escaped beast and the story made such a hit with the circus proprietor that he took our star man and made a press agent of him. Another Sunday night the striking apparatus of a big clock in a church steeple became disarranged and the bell on which the hours were struck boomed out at irregular intervals all night. This was enough for our star man. He sat down and wrote a thrilling story about an escaped maniac who had climbed up in that steeple and was pounding on the bell; and when the paper came out next morning half the police in the city marched down there to capture the madman.

I went to work in the spring, and early in the fall the shakeup my friend of the Sunday paper had predicted came along. He came in as city editor. His first effort at getting in touch with the staff was to assign each member the task of reading the book on journalism he had written. We all had to read it in order to learn how to be reporters, though we considered ourselves about as good a bunch of reporters as the country boasted outside of New York. I never have known why, but that man, who helped me get my job, took a great apparent dislike to me and made me the most miserable young man in the newspaper business. He loaded impossible work on me and hazed me fiendishly.

Finally he got me. One night at midnight, after the cars had stopped running, when there was three feet of soft snow on the ground and the snow was still falling, he came out into the local room and said: "I am sorry, but I have overlooked a very important meeting at Number 94 Yancey Street. It must be covered and you will have to go and get it."

Number 94 Yancey Street was four miles from the office. I asked if I might have a cab and he refused. I started out about midnight and plowed through the snow for those four miles, wet, cold, cursing him at every step. I didn't get there until nearly three o'clock. I rapped on the door of the house. A man stuck his head out of the window. I asked him for the details of the important meeting.

"What meeting?" he asked.

"The meeting about the new railroad that was held here to-night."

"Why," said the man, "we had no railroad meeting here!"

"Wasn't there some kind of a meeting?" I persisted.

"Not that I know of," he said, and shut the window. As I turned away, burning with rage and resolving to whip that city editor next day if I went to jail for life, the man opened the window and said: "Hi, there, kid! I forgot. We did have a small progressive euchre party here to-night, but I don't think it was very important."

I started back, so tired I could hardly walk. Just then the snowplow came along and the good chap who ran it saw my predicament and let me ride up to Main Street with him on it, which was, after all, better than walking.

Next day I went down prepared to club the head off that city editor. I told my closest friend, who had been having it rubbed into him and was willing to help out, but who prudently suggested we wait until after payday, as we might need some money to go to some other town.

That very night, about one o'clock, a fire alarm came in from the lumber-yard district. The city editor rushed out and ordered the short-watch man to go. Then he sent the long-watch man and, at regular two-minute intervals, fired out everybody else. I was about the fifth man out; and I got as far as the first block up the street, where I met a fire-lieutenant I knew, who told me all about it. I came back, wrote the story and turned it in. Meantime the city editor had sent out my chum, who went up to the fire, which was of no account, got the story and walked back. He came in and sat down to write.

"What are you doing?" asked the city editor.

"Writing this fire," he said.

"Huh!" he sneered. "That fire story has been in type half an hour. You didn't seem able to cover it in any decent time and I got another account of it."

"By ———!" shouted my chum. "If this is journalism working here under this man I'll quit now and go and pick gravel with the chickens."

"So will I," I said.

That night we sat up for hours deciding what we would do. We determined to buy a daily paper for ourselves. We knew where there was a paper for sale in a small Western city. And we bought it. I was not yet nineteen and he was barely twenty-one; but we bought it. Youth is impetuous and we were young!

CHAPTER VI

I had been a reporter for eight or nine months, had had my salary raised from ten to twelve dollars a week and had already demonstrated two things to my superiors when my partner and I bought our daily newspaper.

The first was that I had a sort of talent for making friends with and getting the confidence of all sorts of people, from the highest to the lowest; and the second was that I had a sort of talent also for seeing the odd or unusual or humorous side of an occurrence and could write what I saw—rather amateurishly, but well enough to bring out the particular thing that interested me. In other words, I was good —for a youngster—on local color and human interest. Furthermore, I had demonstrated that I hated the routine, was likely to rebel under discipline, had all the cocksureness of youth, would work like a galley slave when a story interested me; but would slide through with the least possible exertion when the story was not to my liking, and that generally I was a rather opinionated and bumptious young person.

It is probable I was a good deal of a trial to my city editors and to the managing editor, but they didn't discharge me; and I was grateful for that, though I felt at times I was not properly appreciated, as every other enthusiastic and ambitious boy does. I was sure I could do the theatres better than the regular theatre man and felt slighted when a big story came along that I did not have a hand in. I was big, healthy, running over with animal spirits and certain I had struck my vocation. There wasn't any doubt in my mind that I could make a great success of that daily newspaper, for I thought I knew it all—and this after seven or eight months at the business, mark you! I jumped at the chance, for in our vealy office talks about newspaper work we had long decided that the only way to make money and reputation was to own a paper—work for oneself instead of for wages. There was nothing in reporting. That was amply demonstrated by the fact that two such colossal geniuses as my partner and myself were working for twelve dollars a week apiece—fully as much as we were worth, by the way—and one or two others on the staff, not half so good, were getting the monumental wages of fifteen and seventeen dollars. The difference between twelve dollars a week and fifteen, when either sum is the total income, is greater than may appear to the casual reader. That extra three dollars meant many things that were unattainable when it did not come in on payday. With a daily paper of our own in a flourishing city, we figured we could easily earn a hundred dollars a week, which meant fifty dollars each; and fifty dollars was as much as the managing editor received—a plutocrat who belonged to clubs and rode in cabs, smoked two-for-a-quarter cigars and had several suits of clothes.

Tad—who was my partner—and I talked until

daylight about the plan. He had had the idea for some time, for an uncle, or a cousin, or a relation of some kind of his, had a paper in a small Western city that he wanted to sell so he could resume the practice of law. Tad outlined the scheme to me. He was to get a few days off, go out to the city, see the uncle, look over the proposition and come back and report. He was sure his relative would give him a rock-bottom price and make easy terms. Also, he was sure his relative would be fair and square, and that this was the greatest journalistic opening for two bright young men—without much capital but with a capacity for work—in the country. I thought so too. Neither of us knew a single thing about any other opening in any other city. Nor did we look for any. We felt this was a providential offering for escape from the bondage in which we were held, and we scraped together enough money to buy Tad a railroad ticket—out and back—and get him a berth each way and his meals. It didn't take a great deal of money, but we had a hard time gathering it. As I remember it, we borrowed about all the available capital of our associates and then had to coax the cashier to advance us five dollars each on our salaries, which was a good deal of a task and took some very fluent and impressive reasons.

Tad left one Tuesday night and I stayed on at work, walking round in a sort of a rose-colored dream and seeing myself a great editor in a great state. I was to be the editor and Tad was to run the business end. Our capacities for these various employments were about equal. I had been a reporter in a small city for less than a year, and he had graduated from college with the idea of studying medicine. Neither one of us knew a bill payable from a passport, and our knowledge of the politics and other local complications of the place we intended to make our home was exceedingly vague. I was not yet nineteen and he was a shade over twenty-one—a powerful combination!

Tad said the reason he wanted me to go into partnership with him was because of my facility for making friends, which gave me a jolt. I supposed this opportunity had sought me out because of my highly developed editorial capacity. However, I was so anxious to show what I could do that I swallowed even that and waited impatiently for his return, occupying my spare time with plans for running the paper. I could see many places where our own paper's methods were deficient and privately I knew the city editor was a dub—and I had my doubts about the managing editor. Our editor was the man I tied to. He could put out a "You-lie-you-villain-you-lie!" editorial, showing how any person who questioned the policies of the Republican party, whether in Washington or the fifth precinct of the Third Ward, or any of the leaders, was a perjured assassin of character; and I read his editorial articles avidly.

The days dragged along until the end of the week. Then I had a telegram from Tad saying he would be in that night. I was at the station to meet him, burning with eagerness to hear his report. I knew all the station people and had no difficulty in getting into the trainshed. Tad looked very important as he came from his car.

"What luck?" I asked.

"Great!" he said.

"Can we get it?"

Could we get it? Oh!—the pathos of that question!

"Yep!"

That settled it. I was to be a great editor. I felt like throwing up my hat and spending the last quarter I had for a telegram to my mother. I didn't, though I borrowed a stamp and wrote her, and used the quarter for sandwiches in the place where Tad and I retired to talk it over. He was stone broke. Indeed, he had lived on a nickel that day, getting a bag of peanuts at a station down the road and eating a few of those every time the dining-car waiter came through with his various calls for meals in the dining car. The trip had cost more than we had planned.

"It's a bully chance!" he told me as we went at the sandwiches. "The city is a fine little place and the paper is all right. My relative wants to go to another city to practice law, and he is willing to make a low price to us for the paper. It is an evening paper. There is another paper there that has been going for twenty years, and a weekly paper; but we can run them out in a short time when we get in there with our knowledge of the business. They are awfully slow and old-fashioned. The paper is four pages and hasn't been looked after. The plant isn't so big as it might be, but we will soon fix that. I like the town. It's a bully little place, and the country round it is prosperous.''

"Has the paper been making any money?" I asked incidentally, for we had talked for an hour of the various editorial reforms we proposed to institute.

"I guess so," he answered vaguely; "for it has got a lot of advertising. It had almost two pages the day I was there. I suppose," he commented, "that is where the money comes from."

"I suppose so," I answered, and then we

went back to our editorial policy. Neither of us was interested in the advertising or circulation, though that was to be Tad's end of it. We talked a long time about the style of the firm—a most important feature—and argued whether his name or mine should come first. Finally we settled it by pitching a penny. I won. My name was to be first and his was to follow the "and," which firm name was to be followed by the words, "Sole Editors and Proprietors."

We stayed there until they shut the place. As we were walking up the street it occurred to me to ask how much the paper would cost. That part of it had been given little consideration. The main thing was to find out whether the proprietor would condescend to sell to us.

"What does he want for the outfit?" I asked in an off-hand way.

"Twenty-five hundred dollars."

Twenty-five hundred dollars! I stopped in the street and looked blankly at Tad. Where would we get twenty-five hundred dollars? For the first time it appealed to me that money must change hands in a transaction of this kind. I hadn't thought of that part of it before.

"Twenty-five hundred dollars!" I shouted. "Why not twenty-five million? Where can we get twenty-five hundred dollars?"

"Oh," reassured Tad, "it isn't all in cash. He will sell it to us for five hundred dollars down and take a mortgage for the rest."

I breathed more easily—though five hundred dollars was more money than I had ever seen at one time in my life.

"Well," I said grandly, "we'll take it."

"Sure!" Tad replied, and we parted to go to our rooms. I walked down to the office and went up to the local room. Two of the boys were on the long watch and the rest had gone. They were reading the last revises. How I pitied them—slaves; mere cogs in a great wheel! While I—I was a Great Editor!

CHAPTER VII

Next day we went into the financial end a little. We thought if we got two hundred and fifty dollars each to make up the five hundred, and a hundred each for expenses and railroad fare and money to have on hand until we could begin to collect on the advertising, we could get along. So we started out to raise the three hundred and fifty dollars each. It was hard work. At the end of two days we wired our benefactor we thought two hundred and fifty dollars would be enough—and two hundred and fifty dollars more at the end of a month. He sent back a "rush" telegram saying that would be all right. This seemed very kind of him. We felt under obligations. We never had a suspicion that his haste might mean anything else but a desire to help two bright young chaps make a start for themselves.

I decided to get three hundred dollars if I could. I soon discovered that three hundred dollars is a mighty sight easier to say and to write than to get—an experience common to everybody who has needed that much money. My rich friends all had excuses. They couldn't quite see the proposition in the bright light I did. Finally I turned to a source that had never failed me in times of dire necessity and the money came, with a blessing. That three hundred dollars was the greatest amount of money I had ever had at one time. It seemed like a fortune. It was a fortune, for with it I was to grab the world and shake from it fame and wealth and power. Tad got some money. I forget how much—but some. Then we both resigned, giving the customary week's notice, and wrote to our benefactor that we would take over the paper on a certain date—about a fortnight ahead.

I left for the seat of my future operations one raw night in March at ten o'clock. The boys came down to see me off. That afternoon one of the city papers had printed a story of the venture. The first line of the head was: "Reporters Become Proprietors." It was a fine send-off. I have the clipping yet. The editor and the managing editor had wished me luck, but had expressed chilling doubts of the success of the venture. The boys of the local staff were frankly envious. They thought it was great.

It was the first long railroad journey I had ever taken and the first time I had ever been in a sleeping car. I watched the other passengers to see how they went to bed and finally turned in. I had the joint capital of the firm, with the exception of enough to bring Tad out a few days later, pinned in the inside pocket of my vest. I wore my vest to bed—an unnecessary precaution, for I was so excited I didn't sleep a wink, but tossed about all night and looked out the windows as we stopped at the stations. Those stops that night are literally burned into my memory. I can call the stations as they occurred until this day; and every time

I ride on that road, which I have done a hundred times since, I look out at those places and that night ride comes back vividly. I can tell the railroad peculiarities of every station we stopped at. Some have new station buildings now, but some have not—and I know them all.

The train crawled. I was anxious to get at the work of being the architect of my own fortune. When we got to the flat country it made me a bit homesick. I was used to hills and valleys. It seemed so bare and depressing. It was a twenty-four-hour journey and the train was more than an hour late, so it was nearly midnight when the porter told me it was time for me to get off. We pulled into a rather pretentious station and the porter took my bag and set it down outside. It was blowing a gale of half sleet and half snow. A hack or two and a couple of hotel busses stood near the station. I took the bus for the hotel Tad had said was near our office and rode up, peering out through the steaming windows to try and see something of the place. I noticed the street lamps were dim and far apart and that there were few lights in the houses. Finally the driver turned into a paved street and rattled up in front of a big, square, slate-colored place he said was the hotel. I was cold and somewhat discouraged. My entry to the scene of my future triumphs lacked many of the features I had pictured to myself.

Five or six men and a dozen women were sitting around a big stove in the middle of the office. I registered and the clerk said he would have a room for me as soon as the troupe that had played there that night left. They were going out on the one o'clock train, he said. Part of them were in the room then, gathered around the stove. I pulled up a chair next to a little, black-eyed, swarthy woman.

She looked at me curiously.

"You leev here?" she asked.

"No," I replied; "but I expect to."

"God help you!" she said, patting my arm in a motherly way.

"Why?" I asked. "What's the matter with this place?"

Then she told me she was the *première danseuse* of the company that had played there that night. They had a spectacular show, with a small ballet in it. Business had been very bad—not only there but elsewhere. The company was about to break up. She had walked about the city. It did not impress her, and the fact that the residents had refused to come out and see one of the world's greatest dancers made it certain to her that the place was of no consequence. She asked me all about myself and I told her.

"Too bad!" she said. "Too bad—and such a nice young man!"

We talked some more. She had been having an incredibly hard time—getting no salary and dancing before unresponsive audiences. If she could only get back to New York! Presently the porter bawled out the train and the actors and actresses bundled on their wraps and crowded into the omnibus. The little *première* patted me on the shoulder again. "Keep enough to get home with," she whispered.

"Good-bye and good luck!" I didn't know it then, but that was golden advice. She waved her hand at me as she stepped into the omnibus. The driver whipped up and the omnibus rattled away. I have often wondered whether she got back to New York—and how. I never heard of her after that.

CHAPTER VIII

The morose night clerk showed me up to my room. It was cold and cheerless. I crawled into bed, but I didn't sleep any that night. I was homesick. All my ideas of becoming a great editor had vanished. I wished I was back on the local staff. I could see the boys reading proof and hear them roasting everybody on the sheet. I could smell the scorched matrices from the stereotyping room; see the foreman cutting the copy into short takes to hurry up the last local and telegraph; could hear the city editor fighting for space and see the foreman grimly shoving galleys of type into the left-over rack. I smelt the hot, inky odor from the pressroom and could hear the whirring of the presses. I was the most homesick young man in the United States!

Next morning, before I had breakfast, the

man who was selling the paper came around to the hotel. He was a tall, cadaverous man, with a sweeping black mustache and a furtive eye. He was very cordial. He sat with me at breakfast and told me how great the opportunity was. The only thing that led him to sell was his love for Tad, whom he wanted to see started in life, and the fact that his profession—the law—was calling for him. He was anxious to close the deal and—did I have the two hundred and fifty dollars with me? I cheered up a lot under his talk and gave him the money, signing some kind of a paper he had prepared. Apparently it made no difference to him that I was a minor and that my signature was of no consequence legally, and I never thought of that phase of the transaction. What he wanted was the two-fifty.

He told me how to get to the office, and excused himself. Later, I learned that he took the first train out of town, leaving me to introduce myself to the employés as one of the new "sole editors and proprietors." He said John, the city editor, would explain it all to me. I was not suspicious. It seemed all right. So, after paying over the money, I bade him goodbye and went to the office.

The place wasn't half a block from the hotel. The former owner said I couldn't miss it. I did, though; and I asked a man where the office of the "Evening Eagle" was.

"Right there," he said, pointing to a one-story wooden building that sat with a gable end to the street and was unpainted, dilapidated and not much larger than our woodshed at home. I stood and stared at it. I had expected to find the paper housed in a brick building of some kind, at least. Still, I remembered Tad had said the plant wasn't much and that one of the first things to do, after the money began to come in under our powerful editorial and business stimulus, was to buy some new presses and type and fix up a business office. I went into the building. It was divided into three parts by partitions. In one room there were an old, flat-topped desk and a tall desk

NEWSPAPER MAN

such as bookkeepers use. In the other room there were another desk and a big pile of advertising electrotypes and a lot of similar junk in heaps on the floor. The composing room was in the rear. It had three or four sets of type cases, a proof press, some galley racks and some other furniture. One man was setting type. He was a small, unshaven man, who chewed tobacco and wore a very dirty collar.

"Hello!" he said.

"Hello!" I replied.

"Want something?"

"I am one of the new proprietors," I informed him with as much dignity as I could command. In reality, instead of feeling dignified, I felt like crying. It was all so different from what I had pictured it.

He laughed—one of those laughs that make you want to kill the man who laughs!

I itched to slaughter him—but I didn't. He was the only person, apparently, from whom I could get any information.

He looked at me pityingly.

"You don't say!" he said. "Well, I'm damned glad to see you, for if we're going to get this rag out to-day we've got to have some copy pretty quick."

"Are you the only person who works here?" I asked him. "Where is the city editor and where are the reporters?"

He laughed again. "He'll be in pretty quick," he replied. "He's gone down to the depot to see if he can't get some of his back wages from the old boss."

I walked out in the other room, sat down in a rickety chair and looked round. It was sickening! Still, I was in for it; and I took some paper, sharpened a pencil and wrote a long editorial article which I headed "Salutatory!" I told the printer to use triple leads, so it would look more important and also take up more space. In this editorial article I informed the citizens of the city of the change of ownership; told of the great capabilities of the new owners; put them squarely on the platform of being for a bigger, better and busier town; promised to fight all municipal and political graft; to bring about much-needed improvements; to hew to the line and let the chips fall where they might; to support all worthy local enterprises; to be unflinchingly independent in politics, choosing for support none but the best candidates—and a lot of similar flubdub. I remarked in capital letters that we had come to stay, had invested our capital here because we believed in the glorious future of the town, and solicited support for our great enterprise from all citizens, stating we would play no favorites but would give the citizens a bright, newsy paper; in fact, I said we intended—and had the capital to carry out the intention—to make this one of the leading papers of the state and a lasting credit to the city.

As I was writing, a man came in. He was a rather shabby man, with a heavy black mustache, and carried an old, faded umbrella, which he gripped tightly in his hand.

He stood uneasily and looked at me.

"What is it?" I asked, rather peremptorily.

"Nothing," he said—"nothing much. Only I'm the editorial staff."

"John!" shouted the printer—"John—dodgast you!—where's your local?"

"Great Scott!" I thought. "That printer seems to be boss round here. I'll soon change that."

"All right, Chet," John replied. "All right. I'll get right at it. Only this man is using my desk."

"I'm the new editor," I said, again drawing heavily on my reserve stock of dignity.

John looked at me the same way the printer had. Then he faltered:

"Am I discharged?"

Fancy a man asking me if he was discharged! Fancy my having the power to discharge any one!

"No, my man," I said patronizingly; "you are not discharged. I shall keep you on until I see what you can do. Of course, if you prove your worth I shall be glad to retain you. At present any arrangement I may make with you is but temporary. I must try you out."

I have thought for many years since that moment that John should have batted me over the head with his umbrella. I deserved it, for I soon found John and that printer were the only real friends I had in that state. John's salary, I may say, was eight dollars a week under the old régime.

"John," squeaked the printer, "did you get any dough out of the old man?"

John hurried into the composing room and whispered to the printer.

"All right," I heard the printer say; "we'll tap him."

John came back to the desk where I was sitting.

"If you don't mind," he said meekly, "I'll write up what local I've got. We go to press at four o'clock."

"Four o'clock!" I shouted. "Do you mean to say you print only one edition in the afternoon?"

"We've always found one enough!" And John grinned a little.

"My dear sir," I said in my most important manner, "that will be changed. We intend to give the people of this city an up-to-date afternoon newspaper. We shall have a noon edition, a home edition and a street edition, and issue extras whenever the news is worth one."

"Well," said John, "that's all right; but you can't start to-day."

"Why not?"

"There ain't enough paper on hand for the edition, for one thing, and the telegraph won't be here in time for a noon edition."

"Telegraph won't be here in time!" I parroted blankly. "Why not? Isn't the telegraph coming in all the time?"

"It comes in by express at two o'clock," said John simply.

"By express!" I was dumfounded. We had the full press report back in the old shop and two specials—to say nothing of cords of stuff from special correspondents.

"Yes," explained John. "Our telegraph is six columns of plate matter sent in from Chicago every morning by express. If the train is late we have to hold the paper until it comes. Once there was a wreck and we couldn't get it out that day at all!"

"Let me see yesterday's paper," I demanded.

John got one. It was a six-column sheet of four pages. On the first page there were two columns of plate matter; then, in the middle, two columns of display advertising; and, to finish up the page, two more columns of plate telegraph matter. There was a column of wishy-washy editorial matter on the second page and two or three columns of plate matter, including the two columns of telegraph left off the first page, and some display advertising. The third page had two columns of local news, set in big type, and advertising; and the last page was mostly advertising of the type called "foreign" —that is, it was patent-medicine advertising and that sort of stuff, and not local advertising. From a casual inspection, judging from the amount of advertising carried, the paper was prosperous if any money at all was being taken in for it.

"I don't like that," I said to John, pointing to the two columns of advertising on the first page. "I shall put that stuff back in the inside of the paper."

"I wouldn't, if I were you," John advised. "That's the only cash advertising we have and we have to give them that position to get the money."

"The only cash advertising!" I exclaimed. "What, in Heaven's name, is the rest of this stuff?"

"I've got to get up my local," said John, and sat down at the desk.

CHAPTER IX

I studied the paper. It was a poor thing. The telegraph news was reasonably fresh, but it humiliated me to think it was cast in plate, shipped from Chicago by express instead of coming in over our own wire. Still, I reflected, it would cost a heap to get wire service and entail the employment of a lot of printers to set the stuff. So I resolved not to cut it off until Tad came, at any rate, and we could talk over wire arrangements and buy a suitable service from the press association. The local news was unspeakable. It was mostly personal items about people who took the trains in the morning, a little sloppy society, a rank story about a meeting of the common council and some stuff about a church fair. "We'll liven that up," I said grimly.

John turned in his local. Meantime another

frowsy printer had come in and taken a case. I found out that the pressman was not due until three o'clock, that we had an arrangement whereby we bought our power from a near-by factory and that our edition the afternoon before was four hundred copies, from which the revenue was considerably less than two dollars. Both Tad and I had forgotten to ask what the circulation was. Still, that made no difference, for we would make the paper so much better than it had been the people would just have to buy it.

It took some tall hustling to get even that small grist of matter put into type. John's copy made me writhe and I edited it as much as I dared. Chet, the printer, told me if I cut out much of it we wouldn't have anything to fill with unless we shoved in some more dead ads.

"Dead ads?" I asked. "What are dead ads?"

Chet took a copy of the paper of the previous afternoon and swept his hand comprehensively over the entire back page and most of the third page, where there was so brave a showing of patent-medicine advertising.

"Them's dead ads," he said.

"What do you mean?"

He laughed again.

"I mean them's ads that the contracts has run out for, and we've bin runnin' them because it was cheaper to use them than set type."

"Do you mean that no money is to be paid for that advertising?" I gasped.

"Not a cent," he said. "Gimme the copy for the rest of that salutatory of yours."

That was a facer. I sat down and read proof on the salutatory; but it was a bad job of proofreading. I could see nothing but "dead ads" in every line instead of the highfalutin language I had so confidently written a short time before.

"Where's the telegraph?" I asked John about two o'clock.

"Down at the express office."

"Why don't they deliver it?"

"Well, you see," said John, "we've been

kind of slow payin' for that stuff and they've gone to sending it C. O. D."

"How much is it?"

John told me and I gave him the money. Presently an expressman came in with a long, narrow box with a sliding cover. In it were six plates, each a column wide, of assorted telegraph news. Chet, who, I discovered was foreman as well as devil, took the six plates, handed me the proof sheet of the plates that were in the box and asked me how I wanted it. There were three columns with display heads at the top and three columns with two-line heads. Thus a big head could be placed in the first, third and fifth or sixth columns, and the other columns sandwiched in between. This slovenly make-up jarred me, but there was nothing else to do. "Anyhow," I thought, "they will all read the salutatory." And if I continued the two-column advertisement in the middle of the page I could have a head on the first column and one on the sixth, and that would make a fairly presentable page. I considered that for quite a time. Then

I told Chet to put the first-page advertising on the inside.

"You'll lose it," Chet said.

"All right," I replied; "then we'll get some more."

Chet laughed again.

After much trouble we got the paper to press. Half a dozen small boys came around about four o'clock and bought a few copies. I took in seventeen cents, which meant I sold thirty-four copies to the boys. That constituted our street sale that day, for nobody evinced enough interest in our enterprise to come in and get a paper—nor did any of the boys come back for more.

The mail came in with a liberal number of exchanges and a lively letter from Tad. I clipped a little miscellany, wrote two or three editorials on broad, general topics and gave them to Chet—and sat down to figure out what had happened.

I couldn't. I felt we had been swindled, but I didn't know enough about it yet to point out.

where. As I was sitting there Chet and John came in.

"Boss," said Chet, "can we have a little money?"

"How much?" I asked.

"A couple of dollars to get something for the house."

I gave each of them two dollars and they left. I found a key in the door and locked it. Then I walked down to the telegraph office and wired to Tad: "Hurry up and get out here. We have been buncoed!"

That night I received a telegram from Tad: "I shall be there day after to-morrow. Cheer up! It's all right."

I was so tired that night that even my fears could not keep me awake; and when I rose next morning and had my breakfast I was in better spirits. "I won't quit," I said. "I'll fight this out somehow."

I went over to the office early and gave John some assignments that opened his eyes. One was to go to the hotels and get a list of hotel arrivals. John turned in this list and I printed it. Next day he came in with a list of notables from all over.

"Get busy, John!" I shouted. "If these people are all here get out and interview them. Ask them how they like the town. Get something out of them and we'll have a few live lines in the sheet, anyhow."

John hurried out, but came back in half an hour looking very sheepish. "It was a joke," he said—"they wrote them names on the register to fool us!"

I had to get the telegraph out of the express office that second afternoon just as I had on the first. Moreover, the man who had the two-column advertisement on the first page came in and said unless he could have that position he would take his advertisement out. "Give it to him," advised Chet—and I did. We needed the money; though when I inquired I found he had that commanding position in that great organ of public opinion for less than two dollars a day!

I took in twenty-four cents from the street boys that afternoon and had an order or two from the carrier routes. Also, I wrapped up the mail myself and sent the papers over to the post-office. Nobody had done that on my first afternoon, but I received no protests. Apparently nobody cared whether the "Evening Eagle" came out or not. Along about five o'clock Chet came in and asked for a dollar.

"Chet," I said, "what sort of a game is this I am up against, anyhow?"

"Well," said Chet, "I'll tell you. I've bin workin' along here for a couple of months and gettin' a dollar or so at a time, an' John's bin doin' the same thing. This here paper was pretty fair one time, but the feller that started it sold out to the man who sold it to you an' moved to another town. This here is a Republican community and the other paper's bin here for years, an' is a good, reliable paper, with a telegraph report by wire, and sticks to the Republican party. They was room enough here for another paper; but the man that just had it threw this here one away from bein' an independent paper an' made it prohibition. Now, that don't go in this here town. He was nasty, too; and he put in a lot of mean stuff about our citizens.

"Nacherally the 'Eagle' lost circulation; an' he was a lawyer an' didn't know nothin' about newspapers, anyhow. The sheriff's bin jist two jumps behind us for two months. Then the editor gets you fellers on the string and sells to you. It was a shame. He rigged up a plant on you. He showed that feller that came out here fake contracts and run the paper full of dead advertising and buncoed him right smart. He was at the end of his string, an' he knew it; an' he jumped the town with whatever money you gave him. Everything here's mortgaged an' we owe everybody in town. The paper ain't worth a damn—an' never has bin; and you're plumb up against it!"

Then Chet took the paper and showed me in detail just how we had been flim-flammed. As nearly as I could make it out, the paper carried about twenty dollars' worth of live advertising a day, with all the rest worthless; and there were no contracts outstanding. We were in debt to the paper house and could only get paper by paying from day to day. Of course I didn't purpose to pay off the old debts; but I didn't know whether Tad had bought the institution, debts and all, or not. I soon found out. He had.

CHAPTER X

Tad came in that night and I went down to meet him. He got jauntily off the train, carrying a guitar-case in his hand.

"What's that?" I asked.

"My guitar," he answered. "I thought we might like a little music of an evening until we get acquainted around town."

"Fine idea," I said. "Great! Unstrap it and play the Spanish Fandango now."

"What for?" he asked in amazement.

"Oh, nothing," I said; "but I sort of need music at this juncture."

"What's biting you?"

"Nothing—nothing at all, except that we're the two biggest suckers on the inhabited globe."

Tad dropped his guitar.

"What's the matter? Isn't everything all right?"

"Tad, I said, "this is no place to break the news to you. Let me lead you to the seclusion of our boarding house. Have you got any more money?"

Tad looked at me blankly.

"More money?" he asked. "Do you think I'm John D. Rockefeller? I gave you all the money I could get. What's become of it? I've only a few dollars in my pocket."

"Come on!" I said firmly. "Come on, before I kill you on the spot! What do we want with more money? Why, dad blame you, we want all the money in the world to pull this thing your benignant relative sold to us out of the hole."

Tad said nothing. As we walked up the street I suggested:

"Play a little something on your guitar, Tad. A little music will be fine while we are getting acquainted."

"Shut up," he retorted savagely, "or I'll break it over your head!"

"That's right," I replied. "My head is thick

enough to break anything on, or I wouldn't be here."

There was no more conversation until we reached the room I had rented. I lighted a cigar a man had given me who wanted a two-column puff of his candidacy for assessor printed for nothing, and Tad sat on the bed and glowered.

"What is it?" he finally said. "Get it out of your system. What's wrong?"

"What's wrong?" I shouted. "Hear him babble! What's wrong? Why, you fair-haired galoot, everything is wrong. Here, we've quit our jobs and come away out here and given a relative of yours—a dear, kind, honest relative of yours—who wanted to see you get a start in the world, two hundred and fifty dollars of good money and tied ourselves up for more than two thousand more, for a rag of a sheet that isn't worth two hundred and fifty cents."

"You must be mistaken," insisted Tad.

"Mistaken!" I roared—"when the total cash receipts of the place for the first four days are less than a dollar; when the total advertising isn't worth twenty dollars a day and most of that we've got to take out in trade; when not a line of new advertising can be secured in the place, for they wouldn't advertise with us if we gave it to them; when the paper has been on the wrong side of everything for the last three years; when we've got only four hundred circulation, and two hundred of that complimentary!" I stopped and laughed.

"What are you laughing at?" asked Tad.

"I was laughing to think of anybody being complimented by getting that sheet!"

"But," said Tad, ignoring the remark, "it carried a lot of advertising when I saw it; and he told me it was making good money."

"Surely it carried a lot of advertising when you saw it, but it was dead advertising. Do you get that? Dead advertising! It was advertising that had been paid for and had run out, and he was carrying it for nothing, because that was cheaper than setting up stuff to fill the space. It isn't worth a nickel a year to us!

And all those contracts he showed you had expired. And the plant isn't worth forty dollars—and we don't own it anyhow, for it's mortgaged. And we have to buy paper day by day and take the telegraph boiler-plate out of hock each afternoon before we can get the paper on the rickety old press. And our total cash capital is less than seventy-five dollars—and we can't raise another cent in this world! And our force consists of two bum printers and an editorial staff that doesn't know its name. And they will shut off our power unless we pay up before the end of the week. And the rent on the shack where we are is due and we are likely to be evicted unless we can stave that off. And—— But what's the use? Play something on your guitar, Tad. We need a little music, don't you think?"

"What shall I play?" asked Tad, who sat blinking at me.

"Oh," I said, "play the Dead March in Saul! That'll about hit things off, I reckon."

What is a roaring comedy now was a fearful

tragedy then. We sat in our room and looked at one another. There was nothing to say. If we had had as much business sense as a pair of three-year-old twins we never should have been in that fix; but neither of us had a grain of that useful—not to say essential—understanding. We were a pair of enthusiastic young theorists; and at that moment not only our doll but every doll in the world was stuffed with sawdust.

We discussed the situation. Every plan we laid ran hard against the same stone wall. It all resolved itself to the question of money. If we had money we could scrabble along for a time. Without money we were helpless; and there wasn't a place in the world where I could get another dollar. Tad was in the same case. So we shook out our pockets. We had less than a hundred dollars between us, and there were bills to be paid and other expenses to be met—to say nothing of wages for our small staff.

"Let's go to bed," said Tad.

There was no good reason for staying up, so

we went to bed; and when we were dressing in the morning Tad evolved a plan. It was this: We were to go down to the office, look into the situation thoroughly, get all the information we could from Chet and John; then follow the man who sold us the paper to the city he was to practice law in and ask him to take the paper back—and give us at least enough of our money for railroad fares to the East. That cheered us. We thought if we put the case fairly and squarely up to the former proprietor he surely would be willing to be fair and square himself. That, I may say, was the final evidence of the fact that neither of us was fit to be at large in the world without a guardian.

We fixed up the paper for the day, writing some perfunctory editorial articles and handing John's local news to Chet without even reading it. Then we called Chet and John in and asked them how about it. John hadn't said much up to that time, but he unbosomed himself then. He told how he hadn't been getting his eight dollars a week regularly; how the paper had been milked until the last dollar had been extracted; how local advertising contracts or agreements had been made for long terms at extremely low rates even for so poor a medium, in consideration of payment in advance, and how we were stuck with those agreements and there could be no money coming in for weeks; how dead advertising had been carried along; and how the paper man and the plate man and the power man and the ink man, and all the rest, had been paid from day to day or staved off if possible. In short, he showed us that we had bought an entirely worthless property and that if we had no money we might as well quit.

CHAPTER XI

We both were confident we could pull out if we had two or three thousand dollars; but we might just as well have needed two or three millions. I didn't know how to get any money, nor did my partner. We had trouble enough scraping together the little first payment. So there we were! We put all these facts in as presentable shape as possible and I started for the city where the man who sold us the paper was living. The place was away up north and there had been a heavy fall of snow. We decided it would be wise to go as cheaply as possible—and I went in a day coach. The weather was bitterly cold and so was the day coach. Along about three o'clock in the morning they hustled me out at a junction and told me the train I wanted would be by at five. I shivered round there until the train came along about six, and at noon I got to my destination. It so happened a merchant in that town was originally from my home village and I went to see him and asked him for the name of a good lawyer. He told me where to go.

I laid my case before the lawyer. We had heard of some sort of a legal proceeding called a *capias;* and I thought that was what I wanted. The lawyer listened gravely and after I had finished and suggested a *capias*—not knowing whether a *capias* was a body execution or a death warrant—the lawyer said:

"Very well; I can apply for such a writ. Of course you are prepared to furnish the necessary bond?"

"Bond!" I gasped. "What sort of a bond?"

"Why, in a proceeding of this sort it is necessary to furnish a bond to indemnify the person against whom the writ issues should the writ not be well taken."

It may be I do not remember the legal terminology correctly, but I do remember he wanted a bond; and I also remember vividly that I couldn't have furnished a bond for five cents. That was a facer.

"Can't we do it without a bond?" I asked.

"No," he replied.

"Very well," I said; "I will go down to my hotel and arrange for the bond and call on you later in the day. I must wire my partner."

As I was going out he coughed inquiringly. I turned.

"My retainer," he suggested suavely.

"Oh, certainly," I said quite grandly. "How much will be sufficient?"

"Well, about twenty-five dollars will do in the circumstances—though ordinarily I would ask a hundred. I feel a deep sympathy for you boys and think you have been shabbily treated; so I shall not charge you much."

Charge us much! He was then charging me about all I had. I took five five-dollar bills from my meager roll of money and handed them to him and he gave me a receipt. I have that receipt yet. It was the only thing I brought home with me.

I stumbled out to the street, dazed. It had suddenly dawned on me that getting back our money and giving back the paper were not such simple problems as they had seemed to Tad and myself. Indeed, I had a glimmer we could do neither thing, which proved to be the case. I went to the hotel and asked about the trains. There was no way to get out until the next morning. So I hunted up the former proprietor. I found him in an office, surrounded by lawbooks. He wasn't busy and he was surprised to see me. I was overcome by my wrongs and cried out: "Give us back our money, you swindler! That paper is no good and you sold it to us on false pretenses! You're a cheat!"

He was a smooth and oily person, that lawyer. He half started from his chair as if to attack me. I hoped he would, for I knew I could whip him. He didn't, though. Instead, he sat back, smiled rather indulgently and said soothingly: "Calm yourself, my dear boy. You are excited. What is the matter?"

I was gulping like a child when I sat down,

wild with rage and seeing red. I half formed a plan to throttle him and take the consequences. Then a feeling of my utter helplessness came over me and I almost sobbed as I began my recital.

He listened calmly. Then he began to talk. He told me we had bought the paper with our eyes open; that we were a couple of kids who expected to find as much in a small city as we had left behind us; that running a daily paper in a small town was a precarious business at the best, and that we should have known it at the start; that he sold on a *caveat-emptor* plan; and that, being a lawyer, and familiar with the laws of the state, he had protected himself; that he would not give us our money back and would hold us to our bargain; and that if we did not fulfill our obligations he would proceed against us legally; and that, finally, if we had taken over a proposition like that, with only enough money to pay the first installment, we deserved to lose! And he wished me a very good day and invited me to begin any legal proceedings I saw fit at the earliest possible moment.

I can see him now as I saw him then—through a mist—sitting at his desk, emphasizing his points by tapping on the desk with a pencil and smiling at my great distress.

I was bluffed out. I had nothing to say. I have often wondered since whether I should have jumped in and given him a licking or taken one. My conclusion is that I showed a little sense by keeping off, for I had but a few dollars and I was in a strange town. I didn't jump in. Instead I shouted incoherently and melodramatically something about getting even with him and stumbled out into the snow again. I sent a wire to Tad telling him I could do nothing, but to keep on getting the paper out until I got back. I arrived at the office on the evening of the next day, to find Tad sitting on the tall desk in the corner thrumming melancholy chords on his guitar.

I told my story. We counted our money. There was less than twenty dollars between us.

My trip had cost almost twenty and the twenty-five to the lawyer had peeled us down to almost nothing. Tad had been obliged to pay something to the power man and to the rent man and to the paper man. Also, Chet and John had demanded a few dollars each, saying they would quit unless they got it. The other printer and the pressman hadn't been in. They didn't know how bad things were. We sat gloomily in the darkness. The "Sole Editors and Proprietors" had been depressed into a couple of heartsick, homesick, hopeless boys.

"What'll we do?" I asked finally.

"What is there to do?" countered Tad dejectedly.

"Nothing."

Tad played a few snatches of a serenade.

"Chop it!" I shouted savagely, "or I'll kick that guitar into splinters."

"Oh, very well," said Tad; "but I always resort to music in times like these. It has a soothing effect."

We both laughed.

"Cheer up!" I said. "We'll wiggle out somehow."

Then we talked it all over, canvassing every possible place where money might be secured, coming back each time to the disconcerting realization that neither of us could beg, borrow or steal a penny.

"Let's give the blamed thing to John," suggested Tad.

"What have you got against John?" I asked.

There was more talk. Finally we went to our room and went to bed. In the morning we walked down to the office together. We had little to say, but we were thinking the same thing—that was how to quit. When we reached the office, the dingy office, with its pathetic equipment and its miserable prospects, Tad turned to me and said:

"Let's quit."

"All right," I replied—and that settled it. Then the boy in me came to the surface. I didn't know how we were going to quit, but I did know I was soon to be relieved of this load—

and I was happy. Tad felt the same way. We kicked the door open and strode into the room. John was sitting at his desk, grinding out his local. Tad and I did a dance around the room; and then, putting our arms on one another's shoulders, we sang, with fine barber-shop chords and close harmony effects:

Round her neck she wore a purple ribbon—
  She wore it in the summertime and in the month of May.
And when they asked her why she wore the ribbon
  She said 'twas for her lover, far away!
    Far away—far away!
    Far away—far away!
    She wore it for her lover, far away!

Then we came in strong with the trombone effect, "Om-te-da-de!" and wound up with a breakdown:

  For round her neck she wore a purple ribbon—
  And she wore it for her lover, far away!

CHAPTER XII

John jumped up and grabbed his umbrella and Chet came in with a column rule in his hand. They thought we had gone crazy. And so we had. We were both so delighted to get rid of the load that we danced and sang for ten or fifteen minutes.

"What's the matter?" cried Chet.

"The matter, Mr. Chester White, of Poland, China," yelled Tad, grabbing Chet by the shoulders and waltzing him round the room—"the matter is that this great palladium of the liberties and organ of the best thought of the community is about to give up the ghost—quit, suspend, go out of business, die the death of a dog, and otherwise have its bright light extinguished. That's what's the matter!" And we pulled the astonished John and the amazed Chet into a circle with us and sang with exquisite tremolo and chromatic variations: "Farewell! farewell, my own true love!"

"Gimme some paper!" shouted Tad. "Gimme some paper, until I indite a few words of burning good-bye to this community!" And he wrote an editorial which he headed, "Valedictory," and which closed with this statement: "If the people of this community remember us as long as we shall remember them they will erect a monument to our memory."

"What becomes of us?" quavered John.

"John," I said, "that isn't the important question. The important question is, What becomes of us! You have a palatial home here, John, supported in regal style on your munificent salary of eight dollars a week. Before we go, John, we shall pay you all we owe you—and probably more—money being no object to us at the present time. Be calm, John; be perfectly calm. Undoubtedly your old boss will be back and he will continue as the editorial staff of this tribune of the people."

Chet took the editorial copy. "I was goin'

to jump the burg, anyhow!" he said. We told him to quadruple-lead the valedictory. Then we discussed ways and means.

John suggested there might be a chance of collecting a few dollars on some of the advertising we had been running. He thought there were a couple of accounts he could get something for. We gave John our blessing and started him out. Then we decided to withhold the paper until late in the evening, so we could get all ready to leave by the night train. That gave us pause. Leave by the night train! How in thunder were we going to leave by a night train! It took money to ride on trains and we wouldn't have any after we had squared our bills and paid our help.

While we were considering this the door opened and a young man came in. "How's business?" he asked.

"Rotten!" we both shouted.

"Same here," he said. Then he told us he had come down from Chicago a time before and opened a broker's office for the sale of stocks and grain. He hadn't made a trade. He was broke and he was going back. That, however, wasn't the object of the meeting. He was a telegraph operator, of course, and as he had no business to do he listened to the gossip on the wire. He had taken off a dispatch that had gone through telling of the death of Henry Ward Beecher. He thought we might like to have it, inasmuch as he gathered we had no wire service. I grabbed it, put a scarehead on it and put it on the first page of the paper that night—double leaded. That was the only piece of real telegraph news the "Evening Eagle" had during the time the "Sole Editors and Proprietors" were editing and proprietoring.

John came back presently. He had scraped up seventeen dollars. We put this with our pile and paid off. We had to pay the plate man when he came round, but we decided to use only the paper we had on hand, which would print about two hundred copies of the paper. I took a few to make my file complete and so did Tad; and when the newsboys came we told them to come back at six o'clock, that we had had an accident to our press. When we did let the paper loose we gave the entire edition to the boys and told them to go out and sell what they could and keep the change.

Tad had been rummaging in the desks. Suddenly he let out a whoop. "Hi!" he shouted. "Here's luck! Here are parts of mileage books our friend left behind."

We examined the books with great interest. We figured them out by the aid of timetables. With one we could go as far as Sioux City, Iowa, and with the other as far as Detroit.

"Which way do you want to go?" I asked Tad.

"I don't mind," he answered.

Neither did I. Sioux City looked exactly as good to me as Detroit, which wasn't very good at that. We discussed this proposition for a time. Tad didn't want to make a decision, nor did I. Really, it was immaterial—except that Tad said he knew a man in Sioux City whom he might borrow a few dollars from until he got on his feet. They had been school friends and Tad thought he was in the coal business. That being the case, I insisted Tad should take the Sioux City book, for I knew nobody there, nor in Detroit; and I might just as well land in one place as the other, inasmuch as I should be without money, practically. Tad wouldn't have it that way.

"Let's jeff for it," he suggested.

"All right."

Jeffing is a game played with type, a printer's method of gambling when nothing else is handy. We went out and got the type and jeffed, best two out of three. Tad won. He took the Sioux City book and that left me the Detroit one. So that was settled.

As the afternoon wore on we paid our bills round town, paid the landlady and the boarding-house keeper and packed our trunks. I sent mine back to the city from which we came, by express, and Tad checked his to Sioux City. When everybody was paid we had but a few dollars left. These we divided equally.

Then we gave the word to the pressman and the last edition of the "Evening Eagle," under the sole proprietorship and editorial management of two boys who at the moment had about twelve dollars in capital, was issued. We read Tad's valedictory with much interest. We thought it looked pretty good. It was in the seventh issue under our management.

When we had given the boys their papers we shook hands with John and Chet, locked the door and solemnly threw the key into a gully that ran near the office. We walked down the street and did not turn to look back at the scene of our failure. I have never known what became of the "Evening Eagle." I don't know whether the man who sold it came back and took it, whether the sheriff got it, or whether the plant rusted out where it was. I don't know whether the paper was continued, or by whom if it was. I don't know what happened and I have never cared to hear about it.

The only communication I ever had from that place since then came a few weeks later. It was from John, and he accused me of taking his old, faded umbrella away with me. Six months later I heard from Tad. He had a job running a coal and wood office on the outskirts of Sioux City. Later he studied medicine and now is a big doctor in an Eastern city.

The trains left almost at the same time that night. We stayed round the hotel until time to go. Then we spent half a dollar each to ride up to the station in a hotel hack. There was another passenger. He was a jewelry salesman who, as he said, "was beating it out of this burg." He had done no business. We didn't know what our friend who sold us the paper might try to do, so we said nothing about ourselves. We knew we should be out of the state in the morning and safe from him, at any rate. I never did go back in that state for seven years. On the way up to the train the jewelry salesman told us that some big railroad shops had recently been moved from the city, giving the place a bad crimp. That was another industrial fact we had neglected to inform ourselves about before we made our plunge. Still, our misfortunes were not the fault of the people. They were kind and hospitable and encouraging. They treated us well. The trouble was that we were two visionary young fools, who started on a ten-thousand-dollar adventure with about four hundred dollars in real money. We deserved all we got.

CHAPTER XIII

I bade Tad good-bye when my train came in and climbed aboard. We had figured the mileage correctly. It lasted to Detroit. Then the conductor firmly told me he would have to have money or another ticket. Inasmuch as I had no ticket and little money, I got off to think the problem over. It was a cold morning, colder than any other morning I have ever known, I think, looking back at it; and the people of Detroit didn't seem interested in my affairs at all. I went uptown and made the rounds of the newspaper offices, thinking to get a job. There were no jobs. At least, there was no job for me, as various city editors told me variously.

I had a big Irish frieze ulster I had bought early in the winter. It saved my life, for I economized on food. As I wandered round Detroit I came on a ticket-scalper's office. I counted my money again. This wasn't necessary, for I knew how much I had. It was less than five dollars. I decided to go to Buffalo, for I had a friend there who would give me enough for a ticket home. I was sure of that. My shoes were good and I spent half a dollar for a pair of arctic overshoes at a second-hand store. I figured I would ride two dollars' worth and walk the rest of the way. I took some stuff out of my grip and checked the grip in the railroad station, thinking to send for it when I was in funds. That didn't cost anything. The man said I should pay when I got it out. I never got it out. It may be there yet for all I know. I stowed my stuff away in my pockets and then went back to the scalper's office. He had a ticket over the Grand Trunk, good as far as London, Ontario. He wanted two dollars and a half for it. I inquired and found the regular fare was about three dollars and a half, as I remembered it. It may have been more or less than that. Anyhow, it was more than I wanted to pay, and I went back to the scalper and offered him two dollars for his ticket to London. He sold it to me.

The train left about half past ten, but I sat in the station for several hours before that time. It was warm there. When the train pulled out I had a comfortable seat in the smoking car, though I had nothing to smoke. Money was too precious to be wasted on such luxuries. The conductor looked at my ticket for a long time. My heart was sick with fear that he would reject it and put me off the train. Finally he punched it and passed on. One of the dreams that comes back to frighten me even now is a vision of that conductor—big, bearded, red-faced, standing with a lantern under his arm turning that ticket over and over and looking quizzically at me. Suppose he had rejected it! The thought scares me stiff yet.

The train ran a little late and it was five o'clock in the morning when the brakeman sang out: "London! All out for London! Ten minutes for refreshments." That meant me, though

I had no idea of getting any refreshments at that particular time. I had slept a little and was feeling pretty fit. I climbed down and followed the crowd into the station. At one end of the big waiting room there was a lunch counter. Most of the passengers made dives for that and ordered coffee and doughnuts or pie. I went over to take a look.

One sleepy man was in charge. He was busy attending to the wants of the passengers. I noticed that the sandwiches and doughnuts and apples and cakes were piled on plates near the edge of the counter and that at regular intervals there were little round apple pies—nice-looking little round apple pies—all brown on top and, where the juice had seeped through the edges, that beloved shiny black that I knew would taste so well. I fingered my few coins. Those apple pies tempted me. And I fell.

I edged in here and there among the passengers and turned sideways to the counter. Then, at an opportune moment, I slipped off an apple pie into the big side pocket of my ulster. I waited a minute. Nobody had seen me—and I edged in again. Before the conductor called, "All aboard!" I had five pies in my ulster pockets—five nice little brown apple pies—and a couple of doughnuts. Of course I stole the pies. That crime hung heavy over me for years; but once, a long time later, when I was up that way on a story I went into that station and handed the astonished lunch-counter man half a dollar. I told him it was conscience money. He thought I was crazy and said so, but he didn't give back the half dollar! I imagine the company didn't get it either.

I stood on the platform and watched the passengers get aboard. The train pulled out. I watched it as far as I could see the rear lights. I reckon I was the loneliest boy in the world at that moment! There I was in London, Ontario, with about two dollars in my pocket and a hundred and fifty miles from the nearest place where I could get any more! I was too proud to telegraph home and I resolved to walk in. Walk in! It was in March, cold and snowy. I knew all that; but I was young and strong, and thought I could manage somehow. My ulster would protect me, and I figured I could make fifteen miles a day and get there inside of two weeks. Besides, I had five apple pies for sustenance and, if worst came to worst, could spend a dime or so for food or lodging.

CHAPTER XIV

I turned back into the station. The night man looked at me suspiciously. I felt again just as I had felt when the conductor scrutinized my ticket. Heavens! I thought—if he should know about those apple pies! He didn't, though. He asked me what I wanted.

"I want to stay here in the station until morning," I explained hurriedly. "The family I am going to visit expected me last night, but I was delayed and I don't want to go up to the house until morning. Please let me sit here. I won't bother anybody."

He was on the point of turning me out, but I pleaded with him so earnestly he finally said:

"All right, kid. Make yourself comfortable. It's against the rules, but I'll chance it. Only you'll have to get out early in the morning, before the day man comes on."

The day man came on at seven o'clock, when it was still dark—and still cold, I may say. He made no move to shove me out and I stayed on, finally persuading myself I had a right to be there, inasmuch as I was waiting for a morning train. Presently the train came in. I didn't go on with it, of course; then I bought a cup of coffee and started down the track. On the way I ate my first apple pie. Coffee and then apple pie may not be the idea of a food faddist for breakfast, but it hit me as being a most excellent combination. Also, as I walked down the track through London, I arrived at the wise conclusion that I must conserve my food resources or go hungry later in the coming days.

Ingersoll is nineteen miles from London and I thought I might be able to get there that day. I started in good form and by noon had reached a place called Waubuno. Then I ate another apple pie. It didn't taste so good as the one I had for breakfast, so I put in one of my doughnuts also. That helped a lot, and I started off for Ingersoll like a professional pedestrian.

My greatest trouble was with my ulster. It was very heavy. If I took it off and carried it I became too cold, notwithstanding the exertion of walking; and if I kept it on I was too hot. I compromised by taking my arms out of my sleeves and letting it swing on my shoulders. Before I reached Waubuno I thought that ulster weighed a hundred pounds; but three miles the other side of Waubuno it began increasing in weight until it weighed a ton. I wanted to throw it away, but knew I should freeze if I did. I lightened my load by discarding most of the things I had kept out of my grip.

The last five or six miles to Ingersoll were slow and painful. My feet began to hurt. My arctic overshoes, for which I had spent half a dollar in Detroit, were holding out pretty well, but they were uncomfortably warm at times. Still, the track was fairly clear and the trains not frequent; I plugged along until, about seven o'clock, I got into Ingersoll. I had been ten hours making nineteen miles and was very tired and very hungry—and I had no place to sleep in sight and no food save an apple pie. I walked through the town. The most hospitable place I saw was a livery stable, where a man was cleaning some horses. I asked if I might sit down by his fire for a time. He said I could. When he had finished his horses he came in and we talked for an hour. He was a middle-aged man, smelling strongly of horses; and he told me he slept in a room boarded off from the hayloft upstairs in the livery barn.

I was so tired and sleepy my eyes kept closing and my head dropping on my chest. Finally, about nine o'clock, he punched me and said:

"Say, boy, I'm going to bed. Where are you going to sleep?"

"I don't know," I answered.

"Haven't you got any money?"

"Not much," I told him, and then let him have my whole story.

"Come on up with me," he urged. "I ain't got much of a place, but you're welcome."

He took me up to his room. It was a small

room, with two bunks in it built against the side of the wall. I turned in in the upper bunk, clothes on except my ulster and shoes, pulled the blankets over me and was asleep in half a minute. He poked me out next morning at six o'clock. "Come on down and help me do the chores," he said, "and I'll try to find you some breakfast."

When I tried to put on my shoes I found that walking nineteen miles through the snow over a railroad track was not so easy a task as I had thought it. My feet were swollen and painful, and I had hard work jabbing them into my shoes. I hobbled down and, after he had told me how to hold a pitchfork, helped him with his work. He went out about eight and came back with a bucketful of coffee and some bread and slices of cold meat. I ate ravenously, thinking to conserve my pies, which I had examined that morning and found to be in fair state of preservation.

He told me Woodstock was the next town of any size; and, by looking at my timetable, I found it was nine miles farther along. About ten o'clock I started. The day was bright and sunshiny and the snow had thawed a little; so the walking was difficult. My feet hurt too. The weight of the ulster was unbearable; so I took it off and made a sort of a pack of it with the belt, and carried it suspended from my left shoulder. Half a dozen times I was on the point of throwing the ulster away, but I had sense enough to keep it. That was about the first time I had a glimmer of sense since I decided to go into journalism for myself. That ulster kept me from freezing half a dozen times.

I crawled along the track, passing one or two little places where the men who were in sight looked at me in a way that said to me plainly: "There's a tramp that ought to be arrested." Nobody molested me and I hobbled into Woodstock long after dark. It had taken me all day to walk nine miles. At that rate I would get to Buffalo along in April sometime. I thought. Woodstock is a nice little town, but there are not many people on the streets on cold March

nights. I walked up and down the main street—
I have forgotten its name, but I suppose it was
King Street, or High Street; most of them are
—looking for a place where I could buy some
food for little money. I had eaten two of my
pies during the day. The idea of eating another
pie for supper made me ill. I had but one left
and was on the point of throwing that away,
but thought better of it and kept it.

I went into a hotel barroom and asked a man
I found there if there was a good, cheap restaurant in town. He directed me to a place
down the street and I got a beef stew for fifteen cents that was hot, filling and, without
any doubt, the best dish I have ever tasted in
my life. Then the sleep problem came. I
needed sleep more than I did food. I could
walk no more. Each foot felt as big as a pumpkin and as hot as a baseburner stove.

The waitress in the restaurant told me there
was a hotel on one of the side streets where I
could get a good bed for fifty cents, provided
I had the fifty. I should have to pay in ad-

vance, she said, for I didn't look very respectable or overburdened with money. I went down to the hotel. It was a clean-looking place, but the man in the office was the grimmest-looking person I ever saw. My heart sank as I walked up to the desk.

"Can I get a room here?" I asked.

"You can," he said with a broad Scotch burr in his speech, "if you have the money."

"How much is it?"

"Fifty cents."

I fingered my coins. Fifty cents would make a big hole in my resources.

"Can't you put me in some back room—any sort of a room—anywhere?" I asked desperately—"and only charge me a quarter? You see," I explained tremulously, "I haven't got much money and I have just got to sleep. I'm in a hard fix; and I'll send the other quarter to you as soon as I get to Buffalo. Please, mister!"

He looked at me coldly. "This is no place for tramps!" he said.

"I'm no tramp!" I argued. "Indeed, I am not. I'm in hard luck, but I'm not a tramp. Come on, now, and be a good fellow. I'll do any kind of work you want me to to make up that other twenty-five cents."

"Where will you be getting your breakfast?" he asked, with some show of interest.

"I don't know or care. Please let me have a bed. That's all I ask."

He looked at me steadily for a minute or two. I must have been a woebegone spectacle. Then he asked, rather irrelevantly, I thought:

'What is your business?"

"I'm a newspaper reporter," and I blurted out the whole story of my misfortunes. He had heard of newspaper reporters and, on the whole, considered them a bad lot. One had come down from Hamilton once to look into the sale of some land he was interested in and had not impressed him favorably. Still, I might be different; and I looked honest. I thought of the apple pie in my ulster pocket and blushed with guilt.

"Can ye write a letter?" he asked.

Could I write a letter! I assured him I was the correspondence king. I probably was the best letterwriter in the world. Then he told me he had a long and important letter to write that was worrying him. It concerned a farm he owned in the back country and if I would promise to talk with him and get his ideas and write the letter in the morning he would give me a bed for twenty-five cents.

I know I cried a little from sheer joy when he told me that. A bed, at that time, seemed to me the acme of human desire! He led me up on the third floor and showed me a good, clean bed in a little room. I was asleep in five minutes. But, Heavens! how my feet hurt!

CHAPTER XV

He rapped me up before seven o'clock next morning. "Come down and have a bite of breakfast before we begin," he said. I hurried through that toilet like a man who has but five minutes to get off a sleeping car. They gave me oatmeal, and bacon and eggs, and coffee, and great slices of wonderful bread and new, sweet butter. It was a feast! I ate until I was ashamed. Then I went out to the office and we took up the work of the letter. He told me what he wanted to say and I made a draft of it for him. That didn't suit him and I made another. Finally I got it as he wanted it and wrote it as plainly as I could for him to copy. By this time it was noon and he gave me my dinner and told me I had better stay until the following morning. I rested all that day, had a great sleep at night and another corking breakfast. When I tried to pay him fifty cents for the two nights' lodging he wouldn't take it. He said my letter had earned it; and he told me how to make a crosscut that would save me some walking and get me into Paris that night, nineteen miles by the railroad track. Some years later, when I had money, I bought and sent to that man the finest brier pipe I could find in New York, reminding him of the circumstances; and his scrawled letter of acknowledgment is one of my treasures.

As I started to Paris I took stock. I had accomplished twenty-eight miles and had spent twenty cents of my money. It was a cold, crisp morning; my feet felt better and I was reasonably cheerful. I tried the road my landlord told me of, but found the walking not so good as on the track and soon went back to the railroad. At noon I ate my last apple pie. I had had a respite and it tasted very good, though its long stay in my ulster pocket imparted a sort of a clothy flavor that didn't help it any.

Those nineteen miles to Paris were long and

weary, especially as the only food I had was the apple pie. It must have been nine o'clock when I got in. A railroad section man let me bunk with him and gave me a big sandwich of corned beef and thick bread. I got a cup of coffee and two biscuits for breakfast and started for Brantford, eight miles away. By this time I looked like a tramp. My face was covered with a bright-red stubble of a beard; my trousers were tied round my ankles with heavy string; my overshoes were badly scuffed out, and I was much wrinkled and mussed. However, by wearing my ulster when I was near a village and pulling my hat down over my eyes, I managed to get through without trouble until I reached Brantford.

At Brantford a constable nailed me. He said tramps were his special meat and he was convinced he had a fine specimen in me. I didn't blame him any; but I talked him out of taking me to the lockup and got on such good terms with him that he told me of a hayloft filled with hay, where I might get in and sleep. Brantford, it seemed, had no accommodations for young gentlemen of the road like myself. Nor was there any place to get anything to eat. I was faint with hunger, but I crawled into the hay, buried myself to the neck and was soon asleep. The man who owned the barn came in early next morning, carrying a tin pail. He fussed round on the ground floor of the barn for a time and then went out. I slid down the ladder, grabbed the pail and vanished. I thought it might be his dinner bucket. When I got a mile away I opened the pail. I had guessed correctly. There was a chunk of boiled beef, some bread and butter and a wedge of apple pie. I threw the pie away.

It was twenty-four miles to Hamilton, a city of considerable size, and it took me two days to make it. The food in the dinner pail kept me going all that day; and at night a farmer let me sleep in his house and gave me some soggy potatoes and fried salt pork and tea for breakfast, for fifty cents. I surreptitiously slipped a few slices of the fried pork into my coat pocket and later transferred them to my ulster pocket. That ulster pocket was my commissary. The fried pork held me until I reached Hamilton, where I was extremely wary about railroad detectives in the railroad yards. I figured that I must be somewhat presentable in that city, for I hoped to find a way to get some money. I found a barber shop near the station, got a shave for ten cents and turned my collar. Then I buttoned my ulster round my neck, threw away the remains of my overshoes and swaggered into the station. I had a look at myself in the glass, and, though my clothes were somewhat rumpled, I didn't look so badly. And I was almost eighty miles on my way.

There was a lunch counter in the Hamilton station. It was more ornate than the one at London, but it had the same sorts of sandwiches on it, the same doughnuts, the same cakes and the same apple pies! An apple-pie Nemesis had me in her fell clutches. A train came in. The passengers crowded up to the lunch counter. I edged in and edged out. When the train was called I had edged in and edged out four times—and I had six nice little brown apple pies in my ulster pockets! I tried to get some sandwiches, but they were covered with paper and stuck, though the apple pies slid into my pockets easily. I guess I was calloused by that time, a hardened apple-pie burglar, for I never did try to pay them back for that lot.

It is in the neighborhood of forty-five miles from Hamilton to Niagara Falls. It took me four days to make that trip, and I had the hardest time of the outing. It grew very cold. I had to sleep in a straw stack one night. They arrested me in St. Catharine's, but the judge turned out to be my friend. He wore a Masonic charm on his watch-chain. I wasn't a Mason, of course, being less than nineteen at the time, but my father was; and I told him that, and told him so convincingly that he not only let me go, but lent me a dollar besides.

I ate those six nice little brown apple pies in the course of those four terrible days, and not much else; for I was saving my money for a shave and a clean collar and a general clean-up at the Falls and a ride in. I didn't know just how I could do all that for a dollar-eighty, but I had hopes. I ate those six nice little brown apple pies; and for ten years after that I couldn't look an apple pie in the face.

My experiences along the road had taught me to go into towns by the back streets and I came into Niagara Falls in just that way. I escaped the police on the Canadian side, got over the bridge all right and walked down to take my first near view of the American Falls. I was standing on the parapet watching the Falls and wondering how much it cost to go to Buffalo by train, when I felt a tap on my shoulder. "Police!" I thought; and as I turned I exclaimed, "Please, sir, I haven't been doing anything!"

The man who tapped me on the shoulder laughed. He was a man from my home town who was a consul at Clifton. He happened to be in Niagara Falls, saw me on the street and followed me.

"What's the matter?" he asked.

I told him. Three hours later I started for Buffalo, bathed, shaved, with new linen and new shoes—and with enough money in my pocket to get me home. Four days after I got home my mother died.

CHAPTER XVI

As soon as possible I began looking for another place. I went down to see my former city editor, but neither he nor the managing editor displayed any enthusiasm about having me rejoin the staff. They told me I had been a fool to quit and go off on a wild-goose chase after editorial fame and fortune the way I did, and I knew they were right, although I didn't care for their method of imparting the truth to me. I visited all the other city editors in the place, but apparently I had not sufficiently impressed myself on the journalism of that locality to make it imperative to secure my services; in fact, they all said they could worry along without me, and they all did.

I was then nineteen, had learned a bitter lesson, and was anxious to return into the business at whatever salary might be offered. I looked back at the days when I had received ten dollars a week and thought that a princely income. Papers in two or three other cities in the state wanted men, I heard, and I applied, but soon learned they didn't need me. I knew I could do as good work as half the men on these papers, if not better, but I couldn't make anybody else think so. Besides, it was summertime and they were letting out men—they said—instead of taking them on. Nobody on earth appeared to have the slightest desire for my valuable services. I tried applying by letter—speaking enthusiastically about my capabilities and vast experience—all the way from Portland, Oregon, to Portland, Maine, and didn't get a rise.

Hence I turned my attention to general literature. I essayed fiction, poetry, special articles and all other branches of that fascinating pursuit. One periodical took a story, promised me ten dollars and didn't pay. After a few weeks I concluded there was no nourishment in that, so with a couple of friends I built a shack in the woods on the shore of a lake a few miles from home and went out there to spend the summer and think things over. Foraging was good, the fish bit well and the problem of living was easily solved. After long reflection I concluded I was a dub and might just as well live out my life in that shack as a hermit. I planned it to the last detail. It was manifestly impossible to be a hermit that summer, for the other boys were with me, there were plenty of young people camping and living in cottages at the lake, and there were dances and corn-roasts and fishing parties and excursions and picnics and other festivities to be engaged in—and, inexperienced in hermiting as I was, I knew that festivities were not compatible with the job. But when winter came I intended to remain there, let my hair and whiskers grow—I could picture myself with a long, flowing red beard—and settle down to hermit out the rest of my pitiful existence.

It was a lively summer. I had a lot of fun at no expense save the exertion of catching fish and garnering other foodstuff. Clothes did not bother me, and except when the girls were along no shoes were worn. I fully decided I was a failure, and had rather pleasant anticipations of long winter nights alone in the shack, with no company but my thoughts and my faithful dog. I didn't have a faithful dog, but I was sure I could find one somewhere. Then on the first of August a man from the telegraph office at the head of the lake came up with a telegram for me. It was from my old managing editor, and said if I wanted to come back and substitute during the vacation season he would give me that place and my original ten dollars a week.

He told me to answer by wire. I didn't do that. I answered in person, arriving there the next morning and forgetting all about my hermit decision. Indeed I think I should have made a mighty poor hermit, and probably it is just as well.

I fell easily back into the old swing and worked until the middle of September. Then the boys were all back from their vacations and the editors told me they were sorry but they had no place for me. I had been frugal during this employment and had saved a few dollars, and I didn't mind dismissal much. I had an idea I wanted to branch out again and had been writing round to several people on the office letter heads.

I had a nibble from a big city in another state. Under most careful nursing the nibble developed into a bite, and on the day I left my substitute job I started for the other city. I didn't know what I should get, but I was ready to tackle anything from leading editorial articles to undertakers and morgue, and had endeavored to impress on that editor my ability to do just that.

I went round to see the man who had asked me to come on. It was on Saturday afternoon. He told me he was busy, gave me a ticket to the theatre and said I should come in late on Sunday afternoon and he would see what he could do. The show was Dixey in Adonis, and had Amelia Summerville playing the Merry Little Mountain Maid. I was all cheered up with the idea of getting work and applauded everything enthusiastically. I was a couple of hours ahead of time at the office next day, and the editor was an hour late, which gave me a creepy feeling. Perhaps he didn't mean it!

He did, though. He came in presently, read his letters, gave some orders and then told the boy to bring me in. He was a kindly man and listened tolerantly to my enthusiastic recital of my experience and abilities. Then he said: "I had expected to put you on the local staff, but the situation has changed"—my heart sank into my shoes at that—"and I cannot spend any more money in that direction just at present. However, now that I have brought you on, I can fix you temporarily"—my spirits rose again in a rush—"and will give you a place as assistant proofreader. The salary will be fifteen dollars a week."

Assistant proofreader! That was worse than I had expected even in my most pessimistic moments. My disappointment showed in my face, for he leaned over and said gently: "I am sorry, my boy, but I don't own this paper. If I did things might be different. I am working for wages here just as the others are, and subject to the whims of the man who pays those wages. Be a sport and take this place, and presently I can fix you."

I gulped two or three times and then straightened up in the chair. "All right," I answered. "When do I go to work?"

"To-night. Report to Mac, the head proof-reader, in the composing room at six-thirty. Good afternoon."

CHAPTER XVII

Mac was a thin, cadaverous man, who had asthma and smoked cubeb cigarettes. He had, in addition to his asthma, a chronic grouch against all editors, reporters, printers and all other branches of the newspaper business, and claimed they would all show themselves as ignoramuses if he wasn't there to catch and correct their errors. He was largely right. Mac had a great deal of information packed into that asthmatic head of his.

The composing room was on the top floor of a four or five-story building, I forget which. The business office and editorial rooms were on the ground floor, and the lofts between were vacant. There was no elevator. I remember perfectly how my footsteps on the stairs echoed dismally through those vacant lofts as I climbed up to the composing room for my first night's work. I wasn't especially cheerful either. It was pretty tough for a rising young journalist, who imagined he knew all there was to know about the business, to be reading proof. Still I had made up my mind I would do anything round that place before I would quit, and I went in and introduced myself to Mac. He looked at me curiously.

"Ever read proof?" he asked.

I told him I had, and detailed my experience in the local room where I began my newspaper work.

Mac sniffed. "Great Scott!" he said, "another stuff unloaded on me by that soft-hearted managing editor! Does he think I am running a kindergarten up here?"

It seemed so to me, but I didn't answer. I held copy all that first night and read revises. Mac was one of the most expert proofreaders I have ever known, and his need really was a copy-holder and revise reader, with a man to jump in and take a few galleys during the late rush. He almost could handle the job alone.

The proofreaders' desks were in the composing room, a lively and interesting place, and there was a good deal of loafing-time in the early hours when copy was slow. From midnight on the proof desk was the busiest place in the establishment.

I made up my mind I might just as well be friends with Mac, who at heart was a mighty good fellow, and I laid myself out to win him. It didn't take long. Mac saw I was a rank amateur, but I had told him how much I needed the job, and he excused my stupidity and errors and encouraged me by saying I had the makings of a proofreader in me. He worked on his first night off after I got there, too, so the job wouldn't fall on me before I knew the ropes, and we became fast friends. Incidentally, Mac taught me a great deal about reading proof and gave me graphic and exact information about each member of the staff. I knew all their weaknesses and all the gossip about them and could tell their copy the minute it came to hand. Some of them were pretty bad and some were

NEWSPAPER MAN 147

good, but it wasn't long before I was convinced I was as good as any of them and only needed an opportunity to prove it.

I had plenty of time to myself, as I got off about four o'clock in the morning and slept until noon, thus having the afternoons for myself. I found a room about a mile from the office. The landlady said I could have it for two dollars and a half a week if I would room with another young man. She brought up the other young man. He was a West Virginian who was studying to be an undertaker, and had the room filled with the tools and textbooks of his profession. He slept at night and I slept in the daytime, so the arrangement worked well, and I gathered considerable information from him about embalming and kindred topics. I couldn't see why anybody should want to be an undertaker and he was at a loss to understand why anybody should read proof for a living, so we started out on a mutual basis of disagreement and got along famously.

My fifteen dollars a week kept me going

nicely, but I was lonely, for I rarely came in contact with any of the men on the editorial staff, except the night editor. They held an assistant proofreader in low esteem anyhow. So my companion on my nights off was the embryo undertaker, who was a fine chap. We went to theatres together and, as Saturday was payday with me and my day off, we indulged in a chop and a bottle of ale afterward and imagined we were rolling high. On Saturdays, too, I smoked my only ten-cent cigar of the week. The rest of the time I smoked stogies that came about seven for ten cents. I found a cheap restaurant where I could get breakfast and dinner for fifty cents a day, and at midnight a man came into the office with sandwiches and coffee. So I saved some money.

I had been working for about three weeks and everybody in the editorial rooms had forgotten my existence, except once when I let a bad bull go through on a revise and heard from it emphatically, when the foreman came over to Mac about midnight and said: "What do you know about this? That stiff that writes the alleged paragraphs for the editorial page hasn't showed up to-night and I'm ready to close that page."

"Close it," said Mac. "It will be better without them."

It so happened that the editorial paragrapher was a nephew of the man who owned the paper and had no ability, but was kept on the paper because his uncle didn't know what else to do with him. He had picked out paragraphing as the softest job on the paper, though real paragraphing is one of the hardest, there being then and now but few writers who are good at it.

Here was a chance for me. "How many do you need?" I asked eagerly.

"Oh, half a dozen or so to make a showing," the foreman said. "Why?"

"I'll write them."

The foreman and Mac laughed. "Go to it," the foreman said. I wrote eight. When they came through in proof Mac read them carefully and said: "Not so rotten." That was high praise from Mac. Next night the nephew came up and asked Mac: "Who wrote the paragraphs last night?" Mac jerked his thumb at me. The nephew took me aside. "Keep it up," he said, "and I'll fix it with my uncle so you get downstairs. I hate paragraphing anyhow. I want to be sporting editor."

So I wrote the paragraphs every night for a week and gave them to the nephew, who copied them and handed them in. Then the managing editor came up. "Who's writing those paragraphs?" he asked. They told him I was. "Quit it," he ordered. "Do you think I'm going to let that lobster get by this way? Chop it, or I'll fire you."

That was a body blow. I hoped the managing editor would recognize true merit and take me downstairs, but he didn't. Still I had plenty to do. The night editor found I knew something about make-up, and he let me make up the early pages while he luxuriated in a place near by. The foreman and the assistant foreman became my firm friends and I found some of the printers were pretty good companions. So at the end of the first month I was reasonably well contented, was getting an insight into composing-room methods that stood me in good stead later, and was sending down a few special articles to the managing editor, some of which he ran in when copy was short.

Then I had a smashing blow in the face. One morning about five o'clock, after work was over and I had been sitting round and talking with Mac and the foreman, I started down the long stairs through the vacant lofts to go to my room. My eyes had been hurting a good deal for a couple of weeks and I had vaguely considered going to see a doctor about them. I was using them hard and continuously under the electric light on the proofs and not taking any too much sleep, for I was exploring the city and trying to find material for special articles. I walked down the stairs and out on the street. Just as I reached the sidewalk all the lights seemed to go out and things became utterly black before me. I couldn't figure out what was the matter, but stood uncertainly on the walk, unable to see at all.

I heard somebody coming out and called, "Who is it?" It was Mac. I told him what had happened. I could hear him muttering under his breath. He took me by the arm and led me to my room. On the way I realized that I had become blind. I couldn't see! I almost collapsed when I got that straight in my head. Mac had been cheering me up all the way.

"Mac," I quavered, "what's the matter with me? Am I blind?"

"Don't worry about that," soothed Mac. "I've seen this happen a lot of times," he lied encouragingly. "A few days' rest and you'll be all right. I'll have the doctor over to see you early in the morning."

Mac led me to my room and helped me undress. He told the student of undertaking to look after me, which he did, and I lay there in total darkness until nine o'clock, thinking it might be just as well to kill myself and have it over with. The doctor came at nine o'clock.

Mac hadn't gone to bed, but had called a famous oculist and came with him. Afterward I learned that grouchy, asthmatic, cynical, sardonic Mac had guaranteed the doctor's bill.

The doctor said the trouble was merely temporary. I needed glasses, and a few days in a dark room would fix me all right. This helped a lot and the student of undertaking stayed with me like a nurse. He quit his studies and read to me and told me stories about his adventures, and Mac dropped in every day with the news of the office. On the fifth day my sight came back as suddenly as it had left me, the doctor fitted me to a pair of glasses and I was apparently all right. That day Mac came in in a state of excitement for him.

"Say, kid," he said, "there's a guy got a paper down in the next state who wants an editor. Here's his name. Write to him and maybe you'll get the job."

CHAPTER XVIII

I wrote and then went back to work. Mac favored me a lot for two or three days. The new glasses worked well and I was getting rapidly into the old stride when, one morning about ten o'clock, the landlady knocked on my door and said there was a gentleman to see me. He came up. It was the man to whom I had written about the editorship.

We talked for a time and he said I seemed to be just the man he wanted. He said there was a big strike on in his town; that he and another man who had been working in the mills had started the paper to take the side of the strikers; that they had plenty of money and that it was a mighty good game.

He said the town was all in sympathy with the strikers and the union, and that the other papers were owned by the corporations; and it was the chance of a lifetime to jump in and grab all the business and circulation in the place.

"But," he said, "before I hire you I want to see what you can do. I notice on the newspaper bulletin boards in town that Jefferson Davis is dead"—he wasn't, it was a false report—"and I wish you would write me a column editorial on Davis, remembering that our city is about half Union and half Confederate. Give him his deserts, but don't slop over on him."

I spent the afternoon writing my opinion of Jefferson Davis for a constituency half Union and half Confederate, and mailed the result to the owner. Two mornings later I received a letter from him containing a railroad mileage book and an invitation to come on and take the job. He said the editorial was great and he regretted that Davis had not died, so that he might use it. However, he promised to save it until the proper time should come.

I asked the managing editor if there was any chance of my getting downstairs, and he said there wasn't at that time; so I quit, bade goodbye to Mac and my friends in the composing room, packed my trunk, had a last chop and bottle of ale with the student of undertaking and took the train on Monday morning early. The owner was at the station to meet me.

"Come on up to my house for dinner," he said. "Then we will go down to the office."

We walked up to his house. As we came in he called up the stairs, "Mary, dear, I've got our new editor here for dinner."

"You have?" replied Mary acidly. "How nice of you! And this washday and not a thing for dinner but vegetable soup and cold meat! You have got about as much sense as a canary bird."

"Don't mind that," he whispered. " I plumb forgot it was washday."

It wasn't so bad as Mary had said. At dinner the owner told me the story of the great strike, how he had started his paper, how much money he and his partner had, how it was doing, and afterward we went down to the office.

It was located up one flight of stairs. As we entered I saw that the outfit was not much better than the one I had owned the year before. I had a chill. Still I found that he had arranged for a condensed telegraph service, that he really had a telegraph wire running into the place and an operator, and that there was an experienced man working as the entire local staff. He had a fairly good press and the business end of it was all right.

The local staff came in and I met him. He was a reporter in hard luck, like myself, but he had had about ten times as much experience as I had. However, the owner made me editor-in-chief and we went at it. The telegraph operator, who wasn't very affluent himself, took the telegraph report, wrote the heads and rewrote the important items, expanding them as much as he could. The local staff and the editor-in-chief got and wrote all the local, the editorial articles, most of the advertising, made up, read proof—in short, we got out the paper. We lambasted the tar out of the criminal corporations that were oppressing the strikers, and had a gay old time. Salary was regular for a time. Then it became wobbly. It cost more to run a new paper than our owners supposed and the corporations were putting on the screws wherever possible. My fifteen dollars a week dwindled some weeks to six and seven dollars and some orders on merchants who advertised. It didn't look good.

One day the local staff threw me over a letter. It was from a man in a Southern city who wanted an editor. "Take it," he said; "I am going north when this blows up."

I went out and telegraphed. I had an answer that afternoon telling me to come on, and next day I quit and started south. All told I had about seventy-five dollars in money I had laboriously saved. When I got to my town I found I was in with another new proposition. There was a big and influential paper in the city and this one had been started by a disgruntled politician who had been kept out of the graft.

This man gave me twenty dollars a week, and my duties consisted entirely in an editorial supervision of the paper and the writing of editorial articles attacking his enemies. We had three reporters and were well fixed in handling the local.

I fussed round for a week getting the lay of the land, and then one afternoon I let go a screamer about the local boss and some of his henchmen. That article certainly did call those persons by their right names. The boss was so tickled with it that he had it put on the first column of the first page and double-leaded. When the paper came up the city editor walked over to my desk.

"Better keep under cover for a few days," he advised.

"Why?" I asked.

"That stuff means shooting down here," he told me, "and they're just as likely to shoot you as not."

That was a contingency that had not appealed to me. There was nothing in being shot, so far as I could see. Nothing happened. The local political reporter told me the politicians growled some, but that was all. Three days later I printed another. At the end of the week we put one out that made the first one look like a tract. By this time I was convinced that all this talk about shooting was a bluff, and I dismissed it from my mind. I was elated, too, for we were getting action. The people began to side with us, and the boss said all we had to do was to keep at it and we would drive them all to their holes.

"That last one almost took the rag off the bush," he exclaimed enthusiastically. "Give them another to-morrow and we'll have them on the run."

Then he raised my salary to twenty-five dollars a week and took me out to luncheon. We walked down the street. As we turned the corner a man stepped out of a doorway, holding something bright and shiny in his hand. I remember looking at him curiously and wondering what the shiny thing was.

"Duck!" yelled the boss, diving for a doorway and tugging at his hip pocket.

I heard a sharp report and something whizzed by my head. It sounded like a big bee buzzing. Then I realized the man with the shiny thing in his hand was shooting at me. I don't remember whether I got into that store through the transom over the door or through the plate-glass window. I got in somehow and landed behind a counter. The boss had unlimbered his pistol by this time and was peppering at the man in the street from behind a soda-water fountain. Each fired five times. They were poor shots. Neither was hit. The man in the street disappeared up an alley and the boss loaded his pistol and took a careful reconnoissance. "Come on," he said to me. "It's all over for the time being. We'll eat now."

I didn't eat anything. It didn't seem time for gustatory exercises. Instead I hurried back to the office. There the local political reporter imparted the cheerful information to me that the gang had decided to "get" this fresh Northerner who had come down there and was abusing them, and that probably I was due to be shot sooner or later. He said they expected to shoot both the boss and myself that day.

The boss was used to that sort of politics, but I wasn't; and after writing a flaming story about the attempt of cowardly assassins to murder in cold blood the fearless publicists who had dared to tell the truth about them, and defying them and calling them many other fancy names to the extent of a column and a half, I decided that I needed a change of air and I took it. Years later one of the men who was in the plot to shoot me told me they only desired to scare me. I told him they succeeded in their desire.

CHAPTER XIX

I had expanded a little, so far as living expenses went, and didn't have as much money when I left as I had when I arrived; but I had enough to get to a big Southwestern city some hundreds of miles north, and I went there. In a week or so I had a place as one of the assistants to the sporting editor of a morning paper. My part of the work was to look out for the amateur ball games and amateur sport of all kinds. I got twenty dollars a week. That place didn't last long. One of the peculiarities of the editor was to discharge the first man in on any morning when the opposition morning paper beat us on a big story. I didn't know that. One morning after I had been there a week or so I came whistling into the office about eleven o'clock. The editor was standing in the middle of the local room, with a crumpled copy of our paper in his hand, on the alert for his victim.

"Get out!" he squeaked. "Get out! You're fired! Get out!"

"What for?" I asked in amazement.

"Don't stand there asking fool questions. You're fired, I tell you! Get out!"

And he stamped back to his room. I waited at the foot of the stairs until the sporting editor came along and then I told him of my experience. "By George!" he said, "I forgot to tell you about the old man. I'm sorry. Where do you expect to go now?"

The sporting editor fixed it so that I got the few dollars coming to me on my second week, and I walked over to the hotel and sat down in the lobby and thought bitter thoughts concerning the injustice of things in general and of that squeaky-voiced maniac of an editor in particular. That got me nowhere. Neither did my applications for work on the other papers. So I decided to go West.

The most convenient way to travel, I thought

was to travel light, so I sold my little stock of personal possessions to a second-hand dealer, keeping my best suit—I had two then—and bought a soft hat and a gray flannel shirt. I sold everything I had except a few handkerchiefs and a change of underwear. Then I visited the ticket scalpers. I found a ticket for eleven dollars that would take me a good long way toward the setting sun, and I bought it. That night I walked down to the office, shook my fist at the editor's room and took the train.

The town I landed in was a railroad centre with two poor newspapers. They didn't want any men. I had about decided to try another trip and beat my way when I got a job as barker for a restaurant near the railroad station. My business was to stand outside the restaurant when trains came in and call the attention of the passengers who got off to the unrivaled collection of comestibles within at cheap prices.

I fixed up a fancy line of vocal allurement for the unsuspecting traveling public and was quite successful in getting them to come in. The proprietor told me I was the best barker he had ever had. Besides, my habits were good and I was always in shape to work. He saved good food for me and, although I was in hourly fear that some one I knew might come along and discover the predicament of a rising young journalist, I had a good time, a clean place to sleep and plenty to eat. Naturally I made friends with the regular customers. A good many of the conductors used to eat there. The town was a division point, and after a month or so the conductors knew me well enough to befriend me.

"Say, kid, said one of them, "what's your idea in standing out here and yelling your head off about this bum grub?"

"Why," I replied, "I've got to do something and this seems to be the only opening here for a bright young man like myself."

"How'd you like to go East?" he asked.

I told him I had come out there to grow up with the country, but, now that he had mentioned it, the East looked pretty good to me and

I'd like to go that way better than anything I knew.

"All right," he said, "hop on my train when I go out to-night."

I hopped on, much to the displeasure of the proprietor of the restaurant, who told me I was ruining a promising career as a barker by quitting him in that way. I rode in state to the end of that conductor's run and he passed me on to the next conductor. This lasted all the way to Chicago, where I arrived sleek and well fed and with money in my pocket. Also I arrived in a sombrero and a pair of tan-colored boots that I had bought from a cowboy who was financially embarrassed at the moment of the sale and was willing to sacrifice these treasures for the wherewithal to procure rum.

There was a man whom I had known as a boy who kept a hotel in that town, and I hunted him up. He was glad to see me and extended the hospitalities of his place to me for as long as I cared to stay. I tried all the newspaper offices, but soon found that Chicago newspaper offices were different from those to which I had been accustomed. I got no farther than the dinky reception rooms in most of them, and had the most emphatic refusal of work from a man who, ten or fifteen years later, gave me a most important position. I rather expected to have no luck and I didn't care much. If worst came to worst I could get another job as barker in a restaurant, or waiter or assistant manager, for I had kept my eyes open and knew a lot of the tricks of cheap eating places.

Once in a while the boys on the old paper wrote to me. I had written to most of them from Chicago. One day I got a telegram from one of the boys on the old paper. "Come on," it read; "the chief says you can have a place on the local staff."

I went on that night, first disposing of my sombrero and tan-colored boots. I hated to do that, but I figured I wouldn't make much of a hit in the old local room in that rig. I knew that from the guying I got on the streets of Chicago. When I arrived the chief told me I could go to work, if I wanted to, for fifteen dollars a week. I grabbed that fifteen. And there I was back again where I started. He didn't know it, and I didn't tell him, but I would have taken ten.

There was a new city editor, a friend of mine and a fine chap. He gave me an opportunity. He handed me good assignments and I progressed rapidly. It wasn't long before I had the introductions to all the big stories and was allowed to write specials when nothing big was stirring. Still I had my troubles. One night about half past six I was sitting in the office, finishing some work. All the other boys had gone to dinner. The telephone bell rang. I answered the call, which was from the police station. The lieutenant said there had been a murder out in the eastern part of the city; that a woman had been found in the cellar of her house strangled, and that the coroner was just starting for the place.

I knew the coroner would have to drive past our office, so I left a note for the city editor telling him I was on the case and jumped downstairs. The coroner came by; I stopped him and he let me ride with him. We reached the scene of the murder in half an hour. The house was a story-and-a-half affair in an outside subdivision of the city, and the building nearest to it was a hundred yards away. The woman had been found by her husband—who was a tinner and had been working on a roof on the same street—when he returned for supper at six o'clock. She had been dragged to a corner of the cellar and strangled by a cloth flour-bag that was wound tightly round her neck.

It was a good story. I had a crack at it before the police got there, and I talked to everybody and got everything bearing on the case. Nobody had seen a man go in or out of the house, but it was apparent that the woman had been killed soon after dinner, for she had been washing that day and her clothes were still in the tub. The husband said she had left the clothes in the tub in order to prepare the dinner and then eat it with him. I discovered, or thought I discovered, that the husband and wife were not on good terms, and that was enough for me. I got back to the office about nine o'clock, bursting with the story, which was the most sensational murder we had had for some time. I told the city editor what I had and he shouted excitedly: "Write every darned line you can! You can have all the space in the paper. And put hair on it!" That meant to make the story sensational, which I was aching to do.

I sat down and went at it, always bearing in mind my instructions to liven it up, and I turned out a dime-novel yarn about that murder. It had hair on it, all right. When I got to the identity of the murderer or to the discussion of motives I was going finely. With the information I had concerning the woman's trouble with her husband I dashed off this gem, while describing the body and its discovery by the reporter and the coroner: "As she lay there, there was an expression on her face that forced the thought that she had been struck by one she loved; not pain, not anger, only surprise and grief."

We all thought that was great when the proofs came down, and it certainly did look fine in full-face type in the paper next morning. Then the afternoon papers came out and each had an editorial condemning the paper for printing an accusation of this kind against the husband, who clearly was not the murderer; condemning the editor who passed it, and particularly telling how many kinds of a fool the reporter was who wrote it. One of the editorial writers went a bit into my journalistic history, to my confusion, and both agreed I was a star-spangled donkey and should be sweeping streets instead of working as a reporter. That started all the "Pro Bono Publico" and "Amazed Reader" letter-to-the-editors boys, and the way they scalped me was sickening. It got to be more of a sensation than the murder itself. Two preachers preached about the "Irresponsibility of the Press" on the following Sunday night, and one of them flayed me alive. The opposition papers printed the sermons in full and the weekly papers took a hack at it. I sneaked round on the back streets for a fortnight. I expected to be discharged, but the managing editor never mentioned the thing to me.

CHAPTER XX

Not long after this I had further proof that the managing editor was my friend. It had been announced that Larry Donovan, who had emulated Steve Brodie and had jumped from the Brooklyn Bridge, was coming to our town to jump over our falls, a feat that had never been accomplished successfully. For six nights I had the assignment, "Find Larry Donovan." For six nights I kept on the trail of Larry, and he did not arrive. On the seventh night I had the same assignment. That night I played pool until eleven o'clock and came back to the office with the usual report that Larry had not arrived. We ran a column of short local jottings each day under the head of "Town Talk," and each member of the staff was expected to contribute five items. My first for that night was "Where is Larry Donovan?"

Next morning the opposition paper informed the city adequately where Larry Donovan was. He was in the hospital, having arrived in the city the night before and made the jump. Any time the city editor sent me upon a special mission after that he wrote down my assignment and after it the words, "and find Larry Donovan."

In about a year and a half things began coming my way. I had my salary raised to eighteen dollars a week and was made baseball reporter and dramatic critic. Baseball came in the summer when the theatres were not running, and there was no baseball when the dramatic season was on. My baseball and theatrical stories were popular with the people, but intensely unpopular with the persons who owned the ball club and the playhouses, for I told the truth about both institutions. I became a personage. When my friends came to town I could pass them into the theatres, and I always was good for reserved seats at the ball games. Also I was making some money by corresponding for out-of-town papers and I considered that my career in journalism was safely begun.

Then there came a state convention to the city. I was put in charge of the story. A lot of out-of-town reporters were there and I knew I had to make good, for these stern critics would see my work every morning, while nobody on the ground would see the stories they telegraphed back until their papers came in by mail, and there would only be a few of these. I had two of the boys to help me and we worked practically all the time. We were doing very well and had even received a word of commendation from the managing editor, until the morning of the day when the nomination for governor was to be made.

There were two or three candidates. I had my story all written, when a man I knew to be in the confidence of the bosses came in and told me it had been decided to name a certain man. I changed my story, put a paragraph at the head of it giving this news and went to bed. Next morning I came early to the office. I felt pretty good. I was the first man in—but one. That one was the managing editor. I found him standing in the middle of the local room with a copy of the paper crumpled in his hand, giving an exact imitation of the managing editor who had discharged me a long time before.

"It's all off," I thought; "I'm fired."

"What do you mean by this?" shouted the managing editor. "What do you mean by making a fool of me in this way? Why did you print that this man is to be nominated when I know that another one is?"

I explained. That didn't seem to satisfy him. He was so angry that he sputtered. Then it came out that at a conference of the bosses the night before it had been decided to nominate a certain other man who was considered most available—he was beaten, by the way. The managing editor had been at the conference.

"Why didn't you tell me?" I asked.

"Get out!" he yelled. "Get out!"

It all sounded familiar. I wondered if all

managing editors acted that way. All real ones I had ever known did, anyhow. I left him in the middle of the floor and stood at the bottom of the stairs until the boys who were on the story with me came along. I told them the story and said I thought I was discharged. They said they'd quit if I was. I told them they probably would, anyhow, but we made that compact and went upstairs to see what was coming out of it.

I went in to the managing editor.

"Chief——" I began.

"What time does the convention open?" he asked—rather irrelevantly, I thought.

"Ten o'clock."

"Well, you'd better be getting over there if you're going to do the story." His eyes twinkled. He certainly was my friend.

In addition to my baseball and theatrical work, I had been writing, several times a week, half a dozen short stories about funny little things I had seen or heard. These we ran under the headline, "Side Lights on Life." I noticed, on reading the exchanges to get baseball and theatrical clippings for the Sunday edition, that a paper in a big city to the west of us reprinted a good many of these short stories of mine. "If they are good enough to reprint, why wouldn't that editor like them at first hand?" I asked myself.

I determined to ask him. So I went up there on my first day off and did ask him. He said he would like to print them first hand if he knew who wrote them. I told him I did. He engaged me to do theatres, hotels, this short stuff and specials and said he would give me twenty-five dollars a week. That was as much as our city editor got. It was wealth beyond the dreams of avarice. I went back, resigned, and in two weeks I was working in the new place.

The editor who gave me twenty-five dollars a week and an opportunity to do the kind of work I liked is the man to whom I largely owe whatever success I may have had in life. Before I came there I had been allowed to do pretty much as I pleased and my writing had not had the benefit of close editing. He was a man who had begun somewhat as I had and had won his way to the top of that big newspaper by sheer ability and hard work. Apparently he liked me, and I know I liked him immensely, and I consider him, to this day, one of the best friends I ever had. At any rate, he took me in hand, held me down to brass tacks, was not at all chary in pointing out my faults—of which I had many—and when I did anything worth while praised that work judicially.

He was a stylist—not a faddist—but a writer who believed in clear and simple English and could write it so well that I used often to wonder if I ever could get the grasp of language that he had. He was strong, virile, and could put more in one paragraph than most of the rest of us can get in a column. Moreover, he had a head packed full of information and knew his city as well as I knew the alphabet. Night after night I have seen him stop at the desk where the city directory was kept and read a few pages of names. The result was that as he looked over every proof he spotted an error instantly, and there was no chance of any misstatement of fact concerning local affairs getting by him. He had a prodigious memory and knew thoroughly all the social, political and business intricacies of the town. He was intolerant of stupidity, but had a strong sense of humor and a vivid appreciation of the interesting and the human.

Practically I was working for him, although I was nominally on the city staff and under the city editor. I was anxious to please and to learn. There were two reasons for this: First, I was twenty-two years old and considered it high time for me to get squared away in the work I had chosen for life; and, second and greater, I was married and had serious responsibilities. Everybody who knew me said that by marrying when I was not yet twenty-one I had proved that I was the same kind of a sentimental fool that I was when I dashed out and bought a daily paper some years before. But I wasn't. My early marriage steadied me, kept me from doing fool things, made me chary of shifting positions, held me where I was until I had a good insight into my trade and kept me keen at my job.

CHAPTER XXI

The city editor didn't warm up to me much at first, although we became good friends in later years. I think he had an idea that the managing editor had no business to project an outside man into his staff the way I was put in. Also my salary was within a dollar or two of his, which may have had something to do with it. When they put the linotypes into the old office a year or so before I changed base, we all learned the typewriter, and I brought mine with me to the new place. I was the first reporter in that city to use a machine in preparing copy and consequently I was an object of considerable interest to all the staff. Now, of course, nearly all newspaper copy is made on typewriters. The introduction of the linotype forced that, because the typesetting machines are so much faster than hand composition and the printers had to have longer "takes" or sections of copy than they could handle in manuscript form—decrease in bulk and increase in legibility—in order to work the machines advantageously.

The paper was a morning paper, and I went to work on a Monday afternoon. My first assignment was the theatres. That night there was to be a first production of a new play. I have forgotten what the play was, but it was by some well-known dramatist of that day and the production was quite an event. They gave me two seats, which were the regular critics' seats, but I went alone, as I knew nobody in the town save a few of the people I had met in the office and my wife was not with me. A very prosperous and pleasant gentleman sat next to me on the aisle, and with him a beautifully gowned and most attractive lady. I knew the paper had four seats for every performance and I figured that this man must be somebody important in the organization.

The man did not go out between the acts, nor

did I, and I overheard his conversation about the new play—which was not a very good play, by the way. The man had a frank manner of talking and used some very apt comparisons. Also he held the same views about the play that I did. Hence on my way back to the office I reasoned thus: That man undoubtedly is high up in the conduct of my paper. He held very decided views about that play. Those views coincide largely with mine. Where they do not coincide with mine his judgment probably is better than mine. So I'll let him criticize the play, as it is up to me to make good here as rapidly as possible.

Wherefore, instead of being a critic of that play I became a reporter, mostly, of another man's criticism, for I was terribly anxious to make a good impression with my first work and I considered that the end justified the means. I wrote a column about the play and it was run under a four-line head. Next morning I was early at the office. Soon after the editor came in the man who sat next to me at the theatre the night before came in also. Before he reached the editor's room he called out: "Who wrote the criticism of that play last night?"

"Here's where I either get it or else don't," I thought, and listened eagerly for the editor's reply. He spoke my name and asked, "Why?"

"Because," said the man, "I consider that the best piece of criticism this paper has had for some time."

Perhaps that wasn't pleasant to me! Five minutes later I was called in and introduced. The man was the owner and editor-in-chief of the paper. Many times after that I wrote pieces he didn't like, and he was always frank to tell me so; but he was my loyal friend and stood by me during the five years of my association with him, as I hope I stood by him and as I always tried to do. He died a short time ago. He was brave, able, manly—a great editor and a great man.

Not long afterward, on a dull afternoon, the city editor told me to go out and rustle a feature story of some kind. "Let's start a crusade," he said; "it's been a long time since we have jumped on anything for fair. You are new here and probably can see things that are nuisances which we overlook because of their familiarity. Start something."

I went out and took a look around. The thing that had impressed me most while I had been in the place was the dirtiness of the manufacturing part of the city, the enormous nuisance of the soft-coal smoke that belched unceasingly from hundreds of chimneys. The city I came from was a hard-coal town. I hadn't walked a block befóre I decided this was the worthy subject of a crusade. I made a few notes and came back and pounded out three screaming columns about this frightful menace to the health and comfort of our citizens.

When I handed in my copy the city editor looked at the first page and chuckled. I didn't know why, for the story was not humorous. It was deadly serious. He ran through the copy and chuckled some more. I puzzled over that chuckle for a long time. When I looked at the proofs I found that he had put a two-column head on it and it was in the paper the next morning yelping after the smoke nuisance like a pack of hounds after a fox. It looked pretty good and I was reading it when the proprietor came in. He walked over to where I was sitting and said: "I suppose you wrote that smoke article this morning?"

"Yes, sir."

"Well, it was a fine article. I imagine you intend to follow it up to-day."

"Yes, sir," I replied, all puffed up.

He smiled at me in that kindly manner of his and patted me on the shoulder. "Well, my boy," he said, "I wish you would restrain yourself until we get our smoke consumers in. If you had observed carefully you would have seen that at present we are one of the worst smoke offenders in the city."

That was all he said, but then I knew why the city editor chuckled.

What a man he was! Three or four years

later, when I was in charge of the news of the paper, one of the police reporters brought in a circumstantial story of a counterfeiting gang that had been operating in our vicinity. He had names and dates. This reporter was a most reliable man. I had implicit faith in him. He said the story was all right and I played it up all over the paper. It was exclusive also. Two days later there came a howl from a man in a neighboring city. His name had been used in the story. He threatened a big libel suit, and I found, after investigation, that he had a case. I went to the owner and assumed responsibility.

"I'm to blame," I said; "I ran the story. The police reporter thought he was all right. What shall I do?"

"Better go up and see what they want," he advised.

I went to the neighboring city, wrangled for a couple of days with the man's lawyers and finally arranged a settlement for a considerable sum of money. I telegraphed to the owner, he telegraphed the money to me and I got a release.

Then I went back and handed him my resignation. He read it, said "Shucks!" threw it in the waste basket and never spoke of the incident again.

I was in Canada one day during my first summer on the paper—Canada always furnished trouble for me—when I ran across a big Liberal political ratification. I think it was a Liberal meeting; maybe it was a Conservative meeting —I have forgotten the exact brand of politics displayed there. At any rate, it was a political ratification meeting. I went down to look the meeting over, not that I was interested in Canadian politics or that my paper was, but I thought that I might get a story.

I got one, there is no doubt about that. The politics didn't appeal to me in the least, but the whiskers of the men at the meeting did. There were more kinds of whiskers worn at that meeting by the sturdy Canadian yeomanry than I had ever seen gathered together at one time. There were whiskers of every variety and of every color, morasses of them, swamps of them, meadows of them, wood limits of them, acres of them—whiskers, whiskers everywhere, and not a barbershop in sight. There were sideburns, brannigans, knockers, mutton-chops, full beards, chin beards, paint-brushes, goatees, imperials, vandykes—every known variety and many that had not before that time been classified.

So I confined my story to the whiskers, mentioning incidentally in the last line that the display had been at some kind of a political meeting. I took up the whiskers in detail and described them, apostrophized them, apotheosized them, laughed at them, admired them, stroked them and ruffled them. I was proud of that story, and they ran it in on the first page. A day or two later a Canadian friend of mine, who read a good many Canadian papers in the course of his newspaper work, came in and said: "Well, you've raised merry hell with that whisker story of yours."

"What's happened?"

"Oh, nothing," he replied, pulling a bunch

of newspaper clippings out of his pocket, "nothing at all, except that all the Canadian papers of the same political faith as the persons at that meeting are roasting the eternal tar out of you for insulting and villifying their intelligent voters, and all the opposition papers are quoting it and calling attention to the kind of rubes that make up that constituency."

He was right. For three weeks he filed clippings from Canadian papers and border papers with me, and the things they said about me were not fit for polite reading. The letter-writing brigade—always strong in Canada—got under way, and it seemed to me that I had insulted the Queen or done some other terrible thing. My editor thought it was a joke, and so it was, but it reacted. I have all the clippings pasted in a book, with the original article leading. The title of the book is Notes on Whiskers. Any time I want to say anything mean about a person I can find inspiration and language in that book.

CHAPTER XXII

For the first year my editor disciplined me pretty thoroughly. He clubbed a lot of writing defects out of me, curbed a lot of foolish enthusiasm, encouraged any good idea I had, let me go to the limit when I was right and held me sternly in check when I was at a tangent. He took me over on the editorial page, where I was directly under his eye, gave me a paragraph department to do and smoothed me out to a great extent. Then when I was beginning to have an inkling of my business he turned over the news end of the paper to me. It was a departure, for before that time the city editor had been supreme in the local end and the telegraph editor in his department. I was made responsible for both ends.

Naturally I was full of ideas. I tried on a good many of them. The editor was tolerant and let me have full swing, and I soon found what would work and what would not. Then the city editor went on the Sunday paper and I took the actual city desk and also kept my supervision of the other news department. I put in a copyreader, the first we had had, and right there I began to grow a little. Also I had had my salary raised several times and was getting along comfortably.

There was one good way of making outside money—to get an appointment as a local correspondent for a New York or Chicago or Philadelphia paper. New York papers were best. The rivalry for these places was keen among the reporters in the city. Usually when a correspondent for a New York or Chicago paper left our town or quit for some reason his recommendation was sufficient to insure the appointment of a new man in that field. Hence, though the managing editors in New York and Chicago didn't know it, there was a cash value to the jobs aside from the money that could be made from month to month. They were legitimate articles of barter. A big paper, that had a liberal news policy and would take a fair proportion of the news offered, was worth a good-sized sum of money as a business proposition.

The first one I secured was the New York paper for which I worked for a good many years later in life. The man who had the job was leaving town and, on consideration of seventy-five dollars in hand paid, recommended me as the person best fitted to succeed him, and I was appointed. Some weeks when news of that section was lively I made as high as fifteen or twenty dollars in addition to my salary. It was a very poor week, indeed, when I could not get in five dollars' worth of stuff. Also I learned there the trick of making alluring "queries." No outside paper, except in the case of most important and late stories, allowed its correspondent to send in the news without first telegraphing to the office, stating briefly what the story was and how many words in the judgment of the correspondent it was worth. These queries were numbered and read like this: "Big fire in factory; fourteen killed; 300"; or "Sensational shooting on fashionable street; well-known people involved; 750"; and the news editor at the other end of the wire would order as many or as few words as he wanted. Naturally no story was underplayed in these bulletins. It was not long before I found out what kind of news the outside papers preferred, and I scheduled that kind insistently whenever there was even a remote chance of getting any space. As a result of the expansion and perfection of the service of the press associations the correspondence item probably is not so important to-day as it was in those days. Then we made a good deal of easy money out of it. Besides, when there was a local story big enough to warrant sending a staff man after it from the outside offices we got pay for helping him.

My editor had been liberal with me and had allowed me to hire good men. I was making about fifty dollars a week when I worked seven days, and I had two men on the local staff who were getting twenty-five dollars each and one who was getting thirty. This man drifted in one day and asked for a place. I gave him a try-out, and hired him. He was the best reporter I ever knew, bar none, and I have known all the good ones in the past twenty-five years. These salaries were large for the town. There never had been anything like it before, nor had there ever been a local staff like that before in that town. It was a compact, reliable and at times brilliant news-gathering machine, and we put out a paper that was excellent in every way. Those were good days.

From a reportorial viewpoint every city editor is the meanest man on earth. He has to be. His job requires it. It is a natural and inherent reportorial tendency to think one's particular work the most important on the paper, to want all the big stories, to protest violently when his stuff is cut or not handled properly—as he thinks—and constantly to howl about the smallness of his wage. He holds the city editor personally responsible for all these things. On the other hand, the city editor is held responsible by the editor for the expense of his department and for the thoroughness of the work of his staff; and inasmuch as reporters are not especially amenable to discipline, he must be rigid and unyielding or he will soon find himself in trouble with the man in the inside office.

I don't suppose I was the pleasantest city editor on earth. I was quick-tempered, arbitrary, inclined to be sarcastic over a failure, and I made the men work hard and long; but I got along fairly well for all that. I think the staff liked me; at any rate I liked the staff. The editor gave me practically a free hand. I could hire and discharge almost at will, and did. Every now and then even to this day I hear things about myself from men I discharged for lapses of discipline or failure or lack of ability. Still that part of it is but a feature of the game. I don't blame them.

Once in a while I wrote a story myself, and I wrote many introductions to big stories. I had a good newspaper style and could see the salient point of a story and bring it out vividly and concisely. Also I had a fair sense of humor and kept the paper lively. I was a stern young person and believed that everything that happened should be printed. One night at midnight the head of the police department decided on a general raid of all the questionable resorts in the city. He made a thorough job of it, apparently for the purpose of satisfying himself just how far he could go. He evidently thought over the matter and concluded that at that time of night, with none of the courts working and with the mayor asleep, he was the czar and he started out to prove it. The result was that in an hour he had three or four precinct station houses packed with an assortment of people that ranged from the highest to the lowest. In newspaper parlance we "ate that story up." I spread it all over the first page of the paper with a three-column head. It so happened that Dean Hole, the English clergyman, was lecturing in the city that night. In the book he subsequently wrote giving his impressions of America he reprinted that headline and cited it as a horrible example of the American newspaper tendency to sensationalism, virtuously reflecting that no English newspaper would have done such a thing. Which probably is the truth, but we did it, and that story was a wonder and stood that town on its head.

This tendency to print all the news got me into hot water several times, for I refused to suppress news that the friends of the owner wanted suppressed just as impartially as I delighted in printing news his enemies didn't want printed. He stood by me, too, and so did my editor; only one day, when I had done some particularly obnoxious thing to a friend of the owner's, the owner came in and asked pathetically, "Great Scott, aren't you going to leave me any friends at all?" That paper was absolutely independent. It had no political affiliations save the broad support of the better principles of the Republican party, and this left the editor and myself—subordinate to him—in clover, especially as the business office couldn't interfere either. Whenever there was a local candidate for office whom we didn't like we said so, not taking any pains to be pleasant about it either. There were no strings on us, and we had a lot of fun and got a good many results.

CHAPTER XXIII

Ours was a big city and yet a small one. Local politics were as intense as in a village; local jealousies interfered with many plans for improvement; local enterprise was at times flamboyant and at times dead. There was one central gathering place—the big hotel—and at luncheon time almost everybody of importance could be found there. Here politics was planned and business was discussed. Also at five o'clock in the afternoon the leaders in the various phases of the city's life generally dropped in. It was like the store in the village. Everybody knew everybody else, for when you got down to it the big outside population did not count much in affairs. The town was a good news town. It was a big railroad centre, a big manufacturing place and held a most important commercial position. Always something was stirring, and in our paper we made the most of what there was.

It was a great five years for me. Along in my fourth year on the paper the owner and the editor gave me the title of managing editor. I thought I had arrived. The first sheet of office letter paper I had with my name on it as managing editor I used for a letter to my father, calling his attention to his gloomy predictions of some years before and asking him to observe what had happened. His observations in answer were pertinent, I may say, and admonitory. They consisted of a short communication in which he dwelt on the dangers of getting a swelled head, pointing out a few symptoms in my own case.

Once, before I left the old town I had been offered a political job there. I was told that I could be deputy county clerk if I wanted to, and that the salary would be two thousand dollars a year. I was getting less than a thousand dollars a year at the time and I was sorely tempted, but I had sense enough to decline. I had seen many other newspaper men leave newspaper work for political places, secretaryships and the like, or to go into business, but I had concluded if I had any future at all it was in newspaper work. Only one other temptation to get out of this line of work came to me, although like all of my kind I was constantly talking in those days of the grind and the lack of future and similar rot. I had made many friends among the managers and advance agents of the theatrical business while at dramatic work, and one of these managers told me that if I wanted it I could have a place at seventy-five dollars a week as advance agent for a good star. I went down to New York—it was my first visit to New York, by the way—looked things over and didn't accept. That was the second time in my life I showed ordinary common sense.

New York is the Mecca of all newspaper men working elsewhere. Park Row is the candle in which many country reportorial moths singe their wings. There were times when I wanted to go to New York right away and I made one or two efforts to do so, for I was ambitious. I had many friends among New York newspaper men, all of whom urged me to get into the game down there, but I stuck and I am glad I did. When I did get to New York I was pretty well equipped for the grueling work there.

Finally what I thought was a big opportunity came to me. A local rich man who had mixed in politics and wanted to mix more bought an afternoon newspaper. He spread himself on hiring men at fancy—for us—salaries, imported an editor and went at the job of securing power for himself through the medium of the newspaper business. A year or so later he started a morning paper and then bought the other morning paper—not ours—and combined it with his own. He had approached me several times with offers of positions, but I had not been responsive.

Almost on the very day my five years ended he made me a proposition that caught me. He offered me the position of editor of his afternoon paper at four thousand dollars a year. This was much more money than I was getting. It was more money than any newspaper man in the city was getting, with the exception of one or two. Besides, since I was eighteen I had been working practically all the time on morning newspapers and sleeping in the daytime, and I thought it would be great to have my evenings to myself. My wife coincided with this view. Except on days off I was only in the house to eat and sleep.

I saw my owner and my editor. They said they couldn't meet the raise, so I took the other place. "I'll have to have a contract for two years," I said to my new employer.

"All right," he replied; "have one drawn up."

I went to a lawyer and he drew up a contract for me. It was iron-clad so far as I was concerned. My new employer signed it without reading it. He was as anxious to get me then as he was later to get rid of me. That contract proved a mighty good thing for me later on.

I hired some of the best men in the city and we started in. We made a good paper. I think all who read it will admit that, but it was not a successful paper. Another afternoon paper had the biggest circulation in the town and still another had the Democratic circulation. Of the four afternoon publications ours remained consistently third in spite of everything I or my men could do—and we worked like slaves. As a result before the end of my first year the owner and I were at loggerheads.

We were constantly embroiled with the other newspapers and always on the losing side in politics. I kept my staff together as best I could, but the owner was constantly growling about the expense. Besides, there was great friction between the staffs of the morning and the afternoon papers, and I wished a hundred times I had not left my old place. I was very unhappy, but I was under contract. I cursed that contract in those days as much as I blessed it later.

Things went from bad to worse. The morning paper was getting circulation and we were standing still. I had a fight on with the morning paper, with the business office, with the proprietor and with everybody else. I tried to pull the paper out, but I couldn't budge it. I was the first man down in the morning and the last to leave at night. We tried guessing contests and many other forms of allurement, but there was no change—our circulation was stationary.

The owner had the merit of being frank in his displeasure. He told me what he thought. I told him what I thought also. One day he sent for me to come over to his office. I went and found him at his desk, glowering at a circulation statement.

"You ain't doin' much," he exploded.

"Not much," I admitted.

"Well, I got to have a change round here. Fire those men an' come back an' tell me you've done it."

He handed me a list containing the names of nine men on my staff. The list included all my friends on the paper and all my best men.

"All right," I said, and walked out. I went over to the editorial rooms, called the men in in a bunch and gave them a week's notice. "You are all discharged," I said—"orders of the boss."

"Have you fired 'em?" he asked when I returned.

"Yes."

"I suppose," he said, "you won't be very comfortable around here now all your pals are gone."

"Not very."

"Well, hadn't you better quit?"

I laughed at him. "I would," I said, "if I could. My sense of moral obligation to you will not allow me to. Besides, I would be sure to get into legal difficulties. Duty calls me and I must obey. I shall serve out my term."

"What do you mean?" he growled.

"Why, had you forgotten my contract? That binds me. I cannot evade the responsibilities of that instrument. I must remain, painful as it is to me and to you."

He scowled. "Let me see that contract," he demanded.

"You've got a copy," I retorted; "look at your own. I'll quit when you pay me the full remaining face value of that contract and not before."

He sent for the contract and his lawyer. It was the first time either of them had read that document. My lawyer friend had done his work well. There was fifteen hundred dollars due, but we compromised on twelve hundred dollars. The next morning I walked out of the place with twelve one-hundred-dollar bills in my pocket, and I never went back. I never blamed him for getting rid of me. I could not make his paper go, nor has anybody else been able to; but I have always blamed him for throwing out the others. They were doing good work and the fault was not theirs. However, all of them were soon provided for, and that, I suppose, was his way.

CHAPTER XXIV.

There was nothing left for me in that city. I went fishing for a time and then went to New York. I thought I was ripe for work down there. However, nobody else thought so to any great extent. One Park Row paper offered me a job at twenty-five dollars a week, but I wouldn't take that, and another managing editor held out hopes for several weeks and then refused to give me a chance. Still I had plenty of money and plenty of good friends in the business and I knew it was only a matter of time.

Some of my friends put me in with one of the state committees to help in the literary bureau, and I wrote miles and miles of campaign stuff commending the hero of San Juan Hill, Colonel Roosevelt, who was then running for governor of the state. The Colonel squeaked through, and my job squeaked out at the identical moment he squeaked in.

Meantime I noticed that a certain magazine was running a series of articles called Great Business Organizations and was detailing the methods of some of the larger corporations. I had been observant while I was working with the committee and had learned a great deal about the business of running a state campaign. It was a business, too, not a haphazard venture, and it had that great business man and politician, Benjamin B. Odell, Junior, at the head of it. So I wrote for that series an article describing the business end of a state campaign, and I submitted it to the magazine.

A few days after the election I was taken on the local staff of one of the New York papers. It was one of the smaller papers. I had measly assignments and made forty-one dollars in ten days. On the tenth day I received a letter from the editor of the magazine to which I had sent my article, inclosing a check for fifty dollars and an invitation to come and see him. I went.

NEWSPAPER MAN

We had a talk. He hired me to work for a newspaper syndicate he had bought and for his magazine. I went back to the newspaper office and quit. They didn't seem to mind.

I stayed with the magazine for nearly two years, getting a good general idea of the business, for I worked in the advertising department, the circulation department and, later, on the editorial side, where in a few months I became managing editor. I didn't get much salary at the start, but I was advanced rapidly and had a chance to do some writing. I had decided to stick to writing. I had had all the desk work I needed, for though I felt I had been successful on the first paper where I had an executive desk, I knew I had failed on the second. Besides I had figured out there was more money in writing—if one could write—than in the executive work. I thought I could write.

One afternoon—it was a holiday, Lincoln's Birthday, I think—I was coming downtown on the elevated road and happened on two friends who were on newspapers in the city. They had a day off, too, and we spent our liberty together. Along about six o'clock one of them said: "There is a big Chinese banquet down in Mott Street to-night. I've got several tickets in my desk. Let's get them and look it over."

We went. I was given a seat at the table next to a big, fine-looking man whom I had met before. He didn't remember it, but I did. He was the man who had so emphatically refused to give me a place in Chicago some years back. I didn't mention that, but talked the best I knew how to my editorial friend. He was then editorial director of the biggest New York paper. The New York grind killed him, but what a whale of an editor he was! One of the friends who went to the banquet with me had been urging me to get back into the game. I had already decided to do so some time before, because stuck away as I was in the editorial rooms of a magazine I missed the grip of active newspaper work.

The editorial director and I went uptown together. We talked a lot. I told him about myself and that I should like to get back into the game. Also my newspaper friends put in a few good words. Next day I got a telegram from him. It said: "I have been wondering since I talked with you last night if there is not some work on our paper you would like to take up. What do you think?"

I thought there was. I went down to see him and he hired me to go to Washington to run the Washington bureau for that paper. He gave me a good, big salary, which increased as the years went on. I was then thirty-two years old and I again felt I had arrived. That time it was true.

CHAPTER XXV

One of the rights guaranteed under the Constitution is that every American shall have full privilege to think and say his own particular business is a poor business and that he would have made a much greater success in any other line of endeavor. Newspaper men exercise this right unreservedly. There never is a gathering of reporters or editors that the talk does not eventually shift round to the lack of reward, the hopelessness as to future, and the general worthlessness of newspaper work as a career. Usually, too, the youngsters are the loudest in condemnation. After a boy has been a reporter for a year he thinks he knows all there is to know about his work, and maybe he does. At any rate he tells you what a barren field journalism is, that it gets a man nowhere, and that for the brains and service required a man in any other profession would make much more money and much more reputation. Men older in the business talk about the same.

Now I do not contend a man can get rich or even well-to-do in newspaper work except as an owner; but I do contend that if a man has an aptness for the business and will take the time to learn it, he can do about as well as if he went into any of the other professions—and have a thousand times more fun. At the start he can do better than he could do in law or medicine or usually in commercial business. The great difficulty with the newspaper business is that experience counts for little or nothing. An experienced doctor or an experienced lawyer or an experienced banker gets better fees and is held in higher regard because of his experience. After a certain stage, experience in newspaper work counts for nothing. The great assets are youth and legs.

One often wonders what becomes of the old men in newspaper work. You will find them stuck away at copy desks, or reading exchanges, editing routine departments or writing editorial articles. If you look round the press desks at a National Convention, for example, where every newspaper has its best men, you will see the gray heads are largely outnumbered by the young men—men about thirty—who in addition to knowing as much about their business as the older ones, have the stamina to do the tremendously hard work.

Granting all this, I still hold that if a young man has an aptitude for newspaper work and will learn his trade, there is no better career in this country or any other than newspaper work. In making this claim I do not arrogate to myself any special qualifications as a judge except these: I was actively in daily newspaper work from the time I was eighteen until I was thirty-nine. I left daily work then because I found a broader field for my writing, a field where I could utilize my experience and such knowledge of men and affairs as I had gained in those twenty-one years. I still consider myself just as much of a newspaper man as I ever was, and entitled to my opinion. My work has covered everything, from a country weekly to the biggest assignments on the biggest newspaper in the United States, which means the biggest in the world. I have played the whole string, and have some thoughts on the subject.

A young man starts in newspaper work as a reporter. That is his apprenticeship. In rare cases a man may start as an editorial writer or as a specialist, but unless he has been a reporter and has learned that end of the work he never amounts to very much. The work of the reporters is the heart's blood of the newspaper. They bring in the news. What they find out and write is what the editorial writer must base his comments on, and woe be to the editorial writer who does not keep in touch with the news staff. He gets to be an academic prig, who invariably forms his own opinions from the editorials he reads in his favorite papers. Real editorial writers never are anything but real reporters, with the privilege of commenting instead of reciting. The old-fashioned commentator, who shut himself up in a coop and spun out theories, is rapidly passing away. He has been lost in the shuffle.

In the newest and most advanced newspaper building in this country, not long completed, there isn't a coop or a cavern or a private room on the editorial floor. Every man who has to do with the editorial end of that paper, from the humblest reporter to the imposing editor-in-chief, sits on one floor, out in the open, each man in touch with every other man. Why? Because the reporters who bring in and write the news are the mainspring of the paper. Because it is essential that every man on that paper shall be in close communication with the scouts who are finding out what that big town is doing and what the world is doing—for the telegraph news is all furnished by reporters also—in order to construct an intelligent and forceful paper that shall contain an adequate presentation of what is happening in the world, adequately commented upon, displayed and handled.

No managing editor or city editor or editor-in-chief of a daily newspaper ever amounted to more than a pedantic whoop who was not at the start a good reporter. There are plenty of them, of course, who never were good reporters, but they are not good editors either. They are imitations of the real thing. Go into any big newspaper office in this country and you will find that the big men in charge served their grueling apprenticeship on the local staff, and usually on the local staff of some paper or papers in much smaller cities than they are working in now. The reporter is the foundation of the game. He is the arch and keystone and the pillars. An editor may be the most brilliant of persons, but he is a dub unless he has a staff to report for him and to him, both locally and by wire.

Wherefore, let us look a little into this question of good reporters. There are two broad classes: The good reporter who can get the news but cannot write it except in an ordinary way and the good reporter who can get the news and write it in an extraordinary way. I have heard legends of good reporters with wonderful noses for news who could bring in stories but could not put them up in decent shape. Every town and every office has had or has now one or two of these rough diamonds. Although I do not want to disparage them any, the reporter who gets anywhere is the chap who not only can find the news, but, having found it, can write it. You will discover that the good reporters who are valuable as news men only are the boys who are and have been for years lingering round at forty and fifty and sixty dollars a week, while the writing chap collects the big space bills.

Writing is just as much of a trade as laying bricks or putting in plumbing. Of course now and then a genius flashes who writes intuitively, but most of the men who are getting the money for writing in this country are men who have learned to write, just as a bricklayer learned to lay bricks. Getting the money may be an inartistic and, perhaps, a crass way of identifying the end and aim of writing, but there are very few people in this country who write for any other real reason. They say they do, but they do not. The boys with the messages to deliver may be sincere about their messages, but they are also concerned about the checks.

The only way to learn to write is to write. You cannot get it out of books or by any other method than by grinding it out, and right here is where the newspaper owners and editors of this country do most to injure themselves and a good many of their men. It is almost the universal custom, especially in the smaller offices where the good reporters come from, to grab a youngster who shows ability and aptitude and has the earmarks of good writing on him, and make some kind of a desk man of him. Thus you will find that the bright boy, who if he were kept at it and properly encouraged would develop into a star writer, is made a city editor or an assistant city editor or some thing of the kind and given an executive position as a reward of merit. Usually he is glad to take it, for it means more salary. That knocks the writing out of him. He is too busy to write, and a man who would have made a good reporter is turned into a mediocre desk man.

Desk men are all right in their way—the papers have to have them. But the man who has it in him to make a good reporter rarely makes much of an executive. Such work requires a different kind of brains. The great geniuses in the newspaper business are the men who have both kinds of brains. They are not so common. Still, if you go over the country and pick out the great executives, the big managing editors, you will find that every last one of them at some time was a reporter, and a good one. Conversely, there are on editorial desks in this country scores of men who would have been good reporters and would have developed into excellent writing men, who are giving out assignments and running papers and only making an ordinary fist at it.

I recognize the great worth of the capable city editor, and managing editor, and news editor. I admit that the good reporter would be worthless without him to handle the copy, to fit it in, to realize its value or lack of value. The good editor complements the good reporter. One is essential to the other. What I do think is that for the man who has no capital but his brains the better end of the newspaper business is the writing end, not the executive end. Passing by all the rewards that may come to the executive, to the great editor, I still hold that for a career, for a satisfactory and satisfying business, the writer has the better of it when you take a large view of the situation.

By the "better end" of the business I mean that the writer who is as good as a writer as the executive is as an executive, or comparatively so, can get almost as much money and can be much happier; have a much wider experience, have a heap more fun, live a more pleasant life, know more people, see more things, get more reputation and beat him a dozen other ways. The mistake the young reporter makes is in trying to get a desk for the vain privilege of having a title, some evanescent authority and a few more dollars a week at the start, and I made that mistake myself. That is the reporter's usual ambition. The young man thinks he is getting on when he is made assistant city editor, or city editor, or dramatic editor, or some other kind of an editor; whereas, if he is a writer, if he has it in him to learn to write, he is really going backward instead of forward.

CHAPTER XXVI

Newspaper work is divided into two parts: the writing end and the executive end—that is, of course, on the editorial side. Many editorial desks in this country are cluttered up with men who should be writers and many men are trying to write who should be executives. The difficulty is to sort them out. The place where so many young reporters fail is in not trying to learn to write, but grabbing a desk when the chance comes to them and trying to make other men write. Learning to write is hard work. It takes years to perfect the good writing mechanic. I do not care how much imagination, how much facility of expression, how many ideas a man may have, he wastes seventy-five per cent. of his effectiveness unless he has learned his trade. After he has learned it is when his imagination, his facility of expression, his knowledge of words, his assortment of ideas come in, and make him not only a good writer but a great writer.

There are hundreds of men writing for newspapers in this country who are not writing so well as they might. Indeed, it is held by many critics that our newspaper writing is not so good as it was. That may or may not be true, but if it is true it is because the men who are in the direction of the newspapers haven't it in them to teach these undeveloped writers their business. Besides, the newspapers of this country are in a way becoming standardized. There isn't so much individuality as there used to be. This is due to a multiplicity of causes, but chiefly to the perfection of the news-gathering facilities and resources and methods of the great press associations that are the backbone of the newspaper. Last fall, as I was coming across Wisconsin, I was told of a place up in the woods where an outlaw was fighting for a dam he had built and was holding up a big posse. It was a big, human-interest story. It is quite likely that ten years ago I should have been sent on that story, and if I had been, I could have called, within one or two, the names of the men from other papers I should have met there. I asked who was up there, and was told the Chicago papers had sent up a man apiece and that the other papers were relying on the press associations.

This may be an argument against newspaper work as a career. I don't think it is, but it may be. In spite of standardizing the papers, in spite of the fact that the big newspapers of this country are coming to be more and more intensely local and somewhat provincial, I still think there is no better career in this country for a young man who has an aptitude for it than newspaper work. If you can do big work you will get big work to do.

To get back to the executive end of newspaper work. On the larger papers all the big salaries, or most of them, are paid to the men who direct the papers. The chaps with the executive brains draw down the money. Notwithstanding that, the writing man can beat them—and the real writing man does. He may not get so much money on the newspaper as the managing editor does, but he has a hundred times the opportunity. Think of what it means! If you develop yourself on a newspaper to be a good writer, if you get the reputation, as you surely will, you have the world by the tail, for it isn't necessary to remain with a newspaper. The whole field of literature is yours. You have learned your trade. You can go out and do what you please, where you please, and there will be no lack of a market. But if you are a managing editor and have not developed the writing side, you must remain a managing editor until, in the inevitable course of events in a newspaper office, you are shoved back by the advent of some younger man with newer ideas and more vim than you have, and there is the beginning of the end. I can point out to you in this country scores of men who once held high editorial positions and are now in minor ones; but show me the writing man who is in health who, having reached as high a place as a writer as these men did as executives, has suffered such reverses—not because of old age or infirmity, but because he has lost his market.

I am not speaking about geniuses. There have been only a few literary geniuses in this country and they are all dead. I mean good, skillful workmen. Why is it that in periodical literature, for example, the same names are constantly recurring in the tables of contents? Not because of office favoritism, as many amateurs hold, but because these are men who have learned their business. They know how to write. They can take an idea and make out of it the kind of a story the editor wants. It is the same in architecture, in medicine, in the law, in any other line of endeavor. The men who do the big work are the men who know how to do it. They had talent to begin with, of course; but they developed that talent by hard work and painstaking application of it.

One reason why the newspaper business is not a good business, seemingly, is because so many men and women go into it as a makeshift and because so many persons who have failed elsewhere adopt it, or have it adopt them, because "it is so easy to write." It certainly has allurements at the start. A bright, capable young fellow who can see things and tell about them can, in a few years, so far as reportorial worth goes, be as valuable to the paper as the much older man who has spent years in the service. Moreover, he can earn more money—at the start, mind you—than his colleague who studied law or medicine, or went into a bank or into a clerkship, or anything like that. It doesn't take long for a bright young chap in any kind of a city at all to earn twenty or twenty-five dollars a week. He can do it in a year or two, no matter how penurious his owner or editor may be, or get it somewhere else. How many young lawyers or young doctors can earn a thousand or twelve hundred dollars in the first year or two of their practice? Not one half of one per cent. of all those who start.

The difficulty is that the advancement, at first

so rapid, gets painfully slow, and after a certain point is reached experience counts for nothing. That is what makes the average reporter think and say that his business is no good. The trouble isn't with the business, it is with him. If he was good enough to make a flying start and go along rapidly he is good enough to go as far as he likes if he will take the trouble to learn. Not many of them do. They are content with the first results, and fall into the rut that sooner or later will lead them to the exchange table or, if they get out, to the political job, the private secretaryship, the press agent's place, or to some other similar line of work. They yelp about the lack of reward in the business and do not try to develop their own capacities.

I am not saying that every man or that even one tenth of the men going into newspaper work can learn to write well, but I am saying that not one tenth of the men who do go into it with that latent talent do so develop themselves. "Sufficient unto the day" is the motto that is the curse of the young reporter. He is getting along swimmingly. He has good work and good pay. He does not progress. At the end of his fifth year he is not writing much better than he was at the end of his first year, when some of the knobs had been knocked off him by his editors and copy-readers. He spends his time sitting round and deploring his lack of opportunity in his calling, instead of making a few opportunities for himself.

The life tends to that. A reporter, by the necessities of his business, is constantly thrown in contact with the big men of his city. Unconsciously he arrogates to himself the habits of mind and, perhaps, the habits of living of those men. He considers himself as good as they are—and usually he is—but he lacks the income. He gets into an inflated style of living and blows up. It is at best a happy-go-lucky sort of a life, but the happiest in it are those who do not pin too much faith on the luck end.

Another trouble with the newspaper game is the jealousy of the men in it. A gathering of newspaper men is like a gathering of soubrettes —few people in it can see anybody but themselves. If any man sticks his head above the universal level of the grass in which all are traveling they all take a clout at that head. Almost all praise is given grudgingly. You'd think to hear them talk that any man who does a big story well did it well by accident, and not by any means so well as it would have been done had the speaker had the chance. They are the greatest gossips in the world, which is natural, for their business is to find out things about people and they cannot print half they find out. Then, too, their mode of life is irregular and they are a sort of people by themselves, for if there is any one thing the ordinary person is mystified about it is the making of a newspaper.

Admitting all this—admitting that newspaper work is disappointing in its rewards; that it is essentially an occupation for young men; that men who get old in it are likely to be shoved aside; that the pay is not commensurate with the labor and the intelligence required; that reputation secured in it is temporary; that the grind saps strength; that the life has a tendency to invite the forming of ruinous habits; that it deprives its follower of an opportunity for social enjoyment; that young men become old in it quickly and that old men become useless; that a single mistake may mean the loss of a position; that business-office rules may prevent truth-telling; that special interests may have to be conserved; that it is the hardest work on earth—I still contend that newspaper work in his country offers an exceptional advantage to the young man who has an aptitude for it.

By aptitude for it I do not mean an abnormally endowed nose for news—most of that sort of thing is fake anyhow—or a tremendous talent for writing. What I mean is that a young man, to make a success of it, must have the strength of will to work unceasingly hard for years, strength of character enough to keep his habits reasonably within bounds, and strength of determination enough to go at his business with the desire to learn it thoroughly, not take it slap-dash and, for that reason, after he has slap-dashed himself out, remain at the thirty or forty dollar level.

No matter how good he is, he will never get rich at it; that side of the business may as well be dismissed from the mind. But he will live a life that is full of interest; he will see all there is to be seen, meet all worth meeting; be a part of all great affairs; exert a weighty influence through his reporting; have a potential power he never will realize, but which will be there just the same; have more fun and get enough to live well on; and, if he has applied himself to the mechanics of his business, has stored in his mind the fruits of his experiences, has conserved the acquaintances and friendships he has made, will be ready to stand aside for the younger man when he can no longer compete with the dash of youth and step immediately into a wider and more profitable and, if possible, more useful field.

The fault isn't with the newspaper business—

it is with the men in it. The rewards are there, just as certainly as they are in banking or in any profession; not so munificent, perhaps, but big enough to satisfy any one, and the life is so much more interesting, so much more varied, the perspective is so much greater, the view is so much broader that the compensations are more than adequate. If you want money keep out. It isn't in the game. But if you want experience, to know life in all its phases, to know men and either make or destroy them, to be in touch with what is happening, go in.

Moreover, it is a better business, a cleaner business than it was. The old days of the frowsy, alleged-bohemian, drunken reporter and editor have passed. The present-day reporter is an honorable, clean, self-respecting man, working honorably and cleanly. There is no business in this country where so much for the public good can be done and is done.

In my opinion newspaper work offers better opportunities, aside from the accumulation of money, for real, serviceable, result-getting labor than any other business or profession a young man may choose. Since I secured my first place, twenty-five years ago, the standards of the men in it, and also of the newspapers, have immeasurably improved. They will keep improving. The work is hard, the pay is not large, but the advantages are many and the opportunities are waiting.

THE END